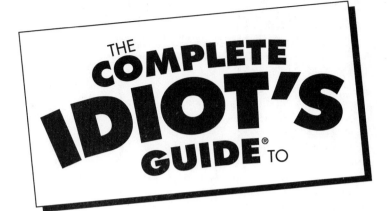

THE COMPLETE IDIOT'S GUIDE® TO

Long-Distance Relationships

by Seetha Narayan

ALPHA

A member of Penguin Group (USA) Inc.

In remembrance of appa, and for my beloved amma.

ALPHA BOOKS

Published by the Penguin Group

Penguin Group (USA) Inc., 375 Hudson Street, New York, New York 10014, U.S.A.

Penguin Group (Canada), 10 Alcorn Avenue, Toronto, Ontario, Canada M4V 3B2 (a division of Pearson Penguin Canada Inc.)

Penguin Books Ltd, 80 Strand, London WC2R 0RL, England

Penguin Ireland, 25 St Stephen's Green, Dublin 2, Ireland (a division of Penguin Books Ltd)

Penguin Group (Australia), 250 Camberwell Road, Camberwell, Victoria 3124, Australia (a division of Pearson Australia Group Pty Ltd)

Penguin Books India Pvt Ltd, 11 Community Centre, Panchsheel Park, New Delhi—110 017, India

Penguin Group (NZ), cnr Airborne and Rosedale Roads, Albany, Auckland 1310, New Zealand (a division of Pearson New Zealand Ltd)

Penguin Books (South Africa) (Pty) Ltd, 24 Sturdee Avenue, Rosebank, Johannesburg 2196, South Africa

Penguin Books Ltd, Registered Offices: 80 Strand, London WC2R 0RL, England

Copyright © 2005 by Seetha Narayan

THE COMPLETE IDIOT'S GUIDE TO and Design are registered trademarks of Penguin Group (USA) Inc.

International Standard Book Number: 1-59257-428-9
Library of Congress Catalog Card Number: 2005929453

07   06   05   8   7   6   5   4   3   2   1

Interpretation of the printing code: The rightmost number of the first series of numbers is the year of the book's printing; the rightmost number of the second series of numbers is the number of the book's printing. For example, a printing code of 05-1 shows that the first printing occurred in 2005.

Printed in the United States of America

Note: This publication contains the opinions and ideas of its author. It is intended to provide helpful and informative material on the subject matter covered. It is sold with the understanding that the author and publisher are not engaged in rendering professional services in the book. If the reader requires personal assistance or advice, a competent professional should be consulted.

The author and publisher specifically disclaim any responsibility for any liability, loss, or risk, personal or otherwise, which is incurred as a consequence, directly or indirectly, of the use and application of any of the contents of this book.

Most Alpha books are available at special quantity discounts for bulk purchases for sales promotions, premiums, fundraising, or educational use. Special books, or book excerpts, can also be created to fit specific needs.

For details, write: Special Markets, Alpha Books, 375 Hudson Street, New York, NY 10014.

Publisher: *Marie Butler-Knight*
Editorial Director: *Mike Sanders*
Senior Managing Editor: *Jennifer Bowles*
Senior Acquisitions Editor: *Randy Ladenheim-Gil*
Development Editor: *Lynn Northrup*
Production Editor: *Megan Douglass*

Copy Editor: *Emily Bell*
Cover/Book Designer: *Trina Wurst*
Indexer: *Julie Bess*
Layout: *Becky Harmon*
Proofreading: *John Etchison*

Contents at a Glance

Contents

Foreword

A long-distance relationship (LDR) is one of the biggest challenges a couple can face. When my now-wife and I had our first LDR, we often said that it would "make us or break us." The physical, emotional, and financial challenges of an LDR put such pressure on you that it will either crush the relationship—or turn it into a diamond.

Sally and my first LDR came when we chose different careers, hers in Boise, Idaho, and mine a 15-hour drive away in Golden, Colorado. For two years, we funneled much of our incomes into the coffers of the airlines and the phone company as we piled up the frequent-flier miles and spent so much time on the phone that I often had to massage the feeling back into my ear.

Our second LDR was much more challenging. I was deployed to Iraq with my National Guard unit just one month after our marriage and 10 months before our first child was born. During the 20 months of this LDR, I missed my wife's pregnancy, heard the first cries of my daughter from a tent at an air base in Kuwait, and saw my daughter growing up only in videos and pictures.

During both LDRs there were certainly some low points, times when either one of us was sure that we could not take it any more. We nearly broke up several times during the first LDR and just simply broke down many more times during the second. Throughout both, though, we continued to have open, honest, and (usually) calm communications with each other, never shying away from being completely frank, even when sometimes the words were angry or simply just didn't come out right. And through both LDRs we continued to look down the road to a time when we would finally be together for good, appreciating each other so much more because of the times we spent apart.

It would have been a great help to have had this book, which provides a road map, direction, and, if you're just starting or contemplating a LDR, many things to consider. *The Complete Idiot's Guide to Long-Distance Relationships* lays out what you can expect from your LDR and solutions to some of the challenges you will face. In these pages you will find a few more bright ideas to make your communications stronger, your interactions deeper, and your times together—whether on the phone, instant messaging, or during those blissful days when you're actually in the same room—more rewarding.

If you are about to embark on your own LDR, I caution you to expect frustration. You will become tired of the travel, of the phone, of simply not having someone there waiting for you at the end of a bad day. But while stressful, an LDR is a proving ground. If your relationship is strong enough to make it through, the end result could be a diamond of your own.

—Chris Chesak

A native of Massachusetts and a graduate of Wesleyan University, Chris Chesak is normally a nonprofit development consultant who lives in Boise, Idaho. Currently he is a machine gunner deployed with the 116th Brigade Combat Team in Kirkuk, Iraq. He looks forward to returning home soon to continue his life with his wife Sally and his daughter Lillian.

Introduction

When Alpha Books offered me a contract to write *The Complete Idiot's Guide to Long-Distance Relationships*, I had just finished seven years of long distance with my husband and was focusing on freelance writing. The book couldn't have come at a better time, and I couldn't have been more interested in writing about the topic. The funny thing is, once one gets started thinking about long-distance relationships—or LDRs, as I'll refer to them throughout this book—the things one can say about them are endless. Try it: ask yourself what wisdom and insights you can offer about long-distance relationships based on your own experience, and you will likely find your mind ranging over a variety of topics, and be surprised at how wise you are.

Well, that's great. That's part of the mission of this book: to remind you of things you already know, or that lie dormant and not articulated in your consciousness. If you're feeling a bit burdened or stressed by your long-distance situation, it's not because you lack insights about it, or lack the resources to make a go of it, but rather because you feel alone and have lost motivation. Well, this book will take care of that problem. You'll meet lots of other LDR couples, too, so it won't be just me cheering you on. In Appendix C, the LDR couples in this book offer words of advice based on their own experiences.

Incidentally, this book is not intended to give the impression that you must handle your long-distance relationship perfectly. You will probably have your screwups and hurdles and learn from your experiences and get better as you go along. Many of the lessons in this book are drawn from experiences of what *didn't* work for various long-distance partners, which induced many of us to think of how we would do things better. Yet despite all our messy experiences, here we are, still with our partners. Obviously, perfection is not a prerequisite for a resilient long-distance relationship—or any relationship, for that matter. The book presents you with a template. Regard it as a friendly resource rather than a set of you-shoulds, and you will do just fine.

Another note I want to add is about gay couples. I struggled to find a writing convention to encompass gay as well as straight LDR couples in my writing. In the end, I settled for saying "he or she" every time I referred to a hypothetical partner, to allow for the reader's sex and orientation. However, all the couples who volunteered to tell their stories to me for this book were straight, and the research on LDRs doesn't delve into any challenges that gay LDR couples in particular face. So there is no special section in this book on the subject. I am acutely aware that there are many gay couples in LDRs. I hope any inadequacies or omissions in my writing will not prevent it from being used by all who can find help and comfort in it, which includes all LDR couples regardless of orientation.

How This Book Is Organized

This book is organized into five parts:

Part 1: "How Long-Distance Relationships Develop," is your introduction to the subject of long-distance relationships. You already know why *you're* in it, but Part 1 can give you language to put it in context for others. Part 1 includes how and why long-distance relationships begin, what precedents we have for such relationships, and whether such relationships are to be considered weird. You'll also meet the couples in this book.

Part 2: "For Better and for Worse," covers the nuts and bolts of the relationship itself: communicating well, fighting well, the cycles of your reunions and goodbyes, advice for LDR parents, military couples, and those who stay up nights worrying about fidelity. Part 2 ends with how to make your LDR stronger over time.

Part 3: "Taking Care of Yourself," discusses how to attend to an entity you probably take for granted: you. Your LDR cannot, of course, do well unless you are well within it. So Part 3 focuses on various aspects on the care and feeding of you. There are chapters here on well-being and sanity, money, traveling, food, and health.

Part 4: "Friends, Family, and the Wider World," tells you how to sustain friendships when you're madly shuttling between two lives, how to stay connected with family and help them to understand your choices, whether or not to mention your LDR at work or at interviews, and how to do it—all these matters you will find addressed in Part 4.

Part 5: "Taking Charge," helps you take a step back and evaluate whether your LDR is working for you and your partner. I show you how to proactively continue in your LDR, if that is your choice when you come to a crossroads, as well as how to seize the initiative to bridge the distance between you and your partner when the time comes.

I've also included three helpful appendixes: In addition to Appendix C, in which LDR couples offer their advice, you'll find a list of books and some helpful online resources.

Extras

You will find the following types of boxes scattered throughout the book, containing tips, pitfalls to watch out for, and other snippets of valuable information:

 Survival Kit
Check these boxes for tips and related information to assist you in your long-distance lifestyle.

 Counting the Minutes
Check these boxes for timesaving tips that can benefit your LDR.

Travel Advisory
Here you'll find cautions and pitfalls to avoid in your LDR.

Go the Distance
These boxes tell you where you can find more information on a topic related to your LDR.

Acknowledgments

I must first acknowledge my husband, Dave. His editing instincts were invaluable to me, and he diligently made the time, even during his lunch hour at work, to read my chapters and send me comments. Many of the insights in this book are his, for I interviewed him many times—probably every time I felt stuck. Next, I must acknowledge Jacky Sach for thinking of me as a possible author for this book, and patiently showing me the ropes in the world of writing and publishing. I am grateful to all the couples who participated in the book. Their names have been changed in the book, so here I'll just use initials: AB, MR, RT, ML&J, PM, KW, KB&RB, JK, MD, RG, CB&RAB, SK, and IK&TK, you know who you are. I hope I haven't left anyone out, and if I have, I hope you will put the omission down to lapsed memory rather than bad intention.

I would also like to thank the people who were willing to share their stories but could not meet my rather stringent deadlines, and whose stories therefore came too late to include. For all the friends and relatives who passed on my e-mails and helped generate stories for this book, I give great thanks.

It has been my good fortune to work with Randy Ladenheim-Gil and Lynn Northrup in preparation for this book, and I am grateful to both for their insights, sensitive way of communicating, and championship of the project in all its stages. My cat, Kala, kept me company throughout the book, snoring away by my desk as I typed, so I must acknowledge him also, as well as Bonnie, my other cat, just for being cute.

Trademarks

Part 1

How Long-Distance Relationships Develop

So you find yourself in a long-distance relationship. Is there a sign on your forehead that says "available for complicated relationships"? No. Is there something weird about you and your partner, surrounded as you are by a sea of single people and couples? Again, no. I'll show you why long-distance relationships, or LDRs, as I'll refer to them, are becoming more common, introduce you to several LDR couples, and show you that there's a precedent for LDRs. It's not like you're starting some new and bizarre relationship ritual.

Chapter 1

Finding Yourselves Apart

In This Chapter

♦ The trend toward long-distance relationships

♦ Why you might be in a long-distance relationship

♦ Meet other long-distance couples

Remember the conversation you had with your partner? It went: "Darling, we can choose something that other couples have not had a chance to choose before." "What's that, sweetheart?" said your partner. "We can choose to be in a long-distance relationship!" you said. "I've always dreamed of it!" your partner exclaimed. "You in one place, me in another, and we keep the love alive on visits!" "Lovely," you said. "Let's sit with pen and pad, and hammer out the pros and cons of it, shall we?"

What rubbish, you are thinking. I never had that conversation. Well, you're not alone. Most couples in long-distance relationships (as they are emerging today) do not plan them. They don't sit and write down pros and cons, and discuss how the LDR—as I'll refer to it throughout this book—fits into a well-organized life plan. The long-distance aspect of the relationship seems to just happen, something people *find* themselves in rather than *seek*.

See if you can find your own long-distance relationship in the following descriptions. After that, we'll meet some real-life long-distance couples. If you don't see your particular story reflected here, don't worry. Certain aspects of long-distance relationships are universal, and you'll find guidance in this book for yours. In this chapter, I'll discuss certain new types of long-distance relationships. In the next, we'll see that LDRs are not all that new.

Hey, Why Is This Happening?

You're part of a trend, despite the fact that your peers and family are slow to catch on. The next time people look pityingly at you, tell them that at least three million couples in the United States alone are in LDRs. Tell them, while you're at it, that LDRs are springing up all over the world. They might still look pityingly at you, but at least there will be an element of doubt in their frank appraisal of you as aberrant. You're not aberrant; faced with a challenge, perhaps. Let's look at some of the reasons you might find yourself in an LDR.

> **Survival Kit** _____
>
> Millions of couples all over the world are in long-distance relationships. There are LDRs among dating couples, young married couples, couples with kids, and older couples—in short, couples in all stages of life.

Opportunities in Different Places

Perhaps you meet your partner in college. You get serious, and maybe you continue dating, or maybe you get married. Then you graduate (at the same time, or not), and it's time to look for jobs. You coordinate your efforts, so that you have a chance to get job offers in the same city. But, lo, the offers, when they come, are in different cities or even states. This happens to academics a lot, but it also happens to people whose skills are specialized. You're qualified for a certain job, but obviously, cannot control where in the country (and sometimes, the world) the openings are. Can you continue your relationship long distance? Of course, never say never. Being bright, talented, and just starting out in your careers, you and your partner are loath to chuck the opportunities. Instead you stay positive, and take the jobs. Maybe you plan to get established in your career so that more options become available later.

Have Brains, Must Use

Maybe you and your partner do the long-distance thing for a while, then bridge the distance and move in together. Or perhaps you stay with your partner the whole time, never even considering long-distance. Either way, you're bright and educated, but put your aspirations on hold to be together. You take a local job, somewhat less prestigious and satisfactory than the job you're qualified for, or you try being a homemaker. Then your head explodes: you need mental stimulation, and don't find it around you. Being massively underemployed is frustrating, and being a homemaker is isolating; you're alarming your partner, the way you clamor for company when he or she comes home. You suspect your potential is shriveling up. Despite your best efforts, you meet no like-minded people who can take the edge off your quandary. Rather than suffer death by tedium, you decide to look for a job that stimulates you, unbound by locality. The job offer you receive is from another state, and your LDR begins.

In both these scenarios, the LDR need not arise from financial necessity. Probably, you could both live on one partner's income. It's the other things—your potential, desire for earning capacity and professional opportunity, and stimulation in a job that excites you—that prompt the LDR.

Married, with Sudden Transfer or Job Loss

You're married, perhaps in a dual-career situation. Or you're married in a one-career situation, with children who are well-entrenched in their schools. Then, you are transferred to a new location. A variant of this situation is when there is sudden job loss. Perhaps, in an uncertain job market, with layoffs common in your field, one day you receive that pink slip. With no job openings in your area, you are forced to look elsewhere for work. It's financially necessary for you to have a job, and when you finally get one, it's far from your family.

There might be many reasons why it's not feasible for your family to move with you. Perhaps you're not sure you'll like the new job, and there's no reason for the family to uproot until you're sure. Perhaps the change is temporary and you plan to return home in a few years, so there's no need for the family to suffer upheavals. Or perhaps your partner and children plan to join you after the kids finish school, or after your partner sells the house and packs up, or wraps up his or her own projects. You discuss all the pros and cons with your partner, and decide it's best for just one of you to move for the moment. Thus, your LDR begins.

Single and Single-Minded

Through college and beyond, you focus on your career goals. You're good at what you do. These are your productive career years, and you know it. You want to establish yourself, and you're having a ball. Maybe you have a marriage (with or without kids), or a couple of relationships, behind you. You're interested in having a relationship again. In one sense, your options for meeting people may have become more limited: everyone around you seems to be paired up, and not know eligible singles to whom they can introduce you. At the same time, your social horizons have expanded: you travel more for work and play, and meet interesting people this way. You can also meet people online, and try it. On one of those travels, or on one of those online chats, you meet someone with whom you bond and who brings you joy, and it's obvious the feeling is mutual. This doesn't mean you're about to quit work. You might still be feeling out the prospects for the relationship. The relationship begins, and continues, as an LDR.

Older and Ready to Stretch

You have children, but they don't need your constant presence anymore. Maybe they've flown the coop and have homes and families of their own. Well, then, you can stretch a bit: for many years, you've held back your potential for the sake of the family. So with your partner's blessing and encouragement—you both feel it's your turn now—you re-enter the work force. Perhaps there's also a financial need for this, thanks to an expected drop in your income after one of you retires. You go back to school for retraining, or just look for a job, locally and in surrounding areas. I'll apply for these jobs, you think; I don't have to take them. Well, you're a bit taken by surprise when the job offer comes from a place several miles, towns, states, or even countries away. You wonder what to do next. The opportunity is a good one, and you feel it should not be passed up. You have many years of marriage behind you, and you and your partner trust each other. You decide you can do it, and thus begin your LDR.

This Job Involves Travel?

When you and your partner hunkered down to make a life together, who knew that one partner would be away for one out of every four weeks? Not you. It could come as a surprise to both of you, this LDR, when you might not even be in a dual-career situation: one of you may be a homemaker. These days, many married Reservists and National Guardsmen called to serve are experiencing just such situations; but there are also people in perfectly ordinary jobs, surprised to find that the job suddenly involves much travel; enough, in fact, to turn the relationship into an LDR.

> **Go the Distance**
>
> New kinds of long-distance relationships emerge when couples have prior commitments to dual careers, meet while traveling or online, decide that one partner wants to get back in the workforce after several years of marriage, or have jobs that require more travel than expected.

Meet Other Couples in Long-Distance Relationships

Let's meet some LDR couples. You'll find snippets of their experiences and insights peppered throughout the book, as well as advice directly from them to you in Appendix C. All of them contacted me to share their stories, and I am grateful to them for their articulation, friendliness, and willingness to reflect on their experiences. As mentioned earlier, many aspects of the long-distance relationship are universal, so even if you do not find your particular story here, you'll receive help and guidance for your relationship throughout this book.

Dan and Erica

Dan and Erica met on a blind date when Dan visited Erica's town. Dan worked as an engineer in Illinois, and Erica as a teacher in Colorado. He was in his thirties, and she in her twenties. One thing followed another, and soon they were in an LDR. Contact was primarily over the phone: they couldn't afford more than a couple of trips a year. Finally, Dan chucked his job and moved to Colorado to join her. They have been married for several years.

Pam and John

Pam is a 60-year-old medical consultant with a demanding travel job that takes her from city to city every three months. Her husband, John, is 70 and retired from a sports management job. They live in Arizona. Pam stays in a hotel Sunday night through Thursday evening, and returns home for the weekend. She has been maintaining this schedule for over five years.

Marina and Josh

Marina, 26, and Josh, 24, met in junior high in Colorado when she was in tenth grade, and he in the eighth. They dated and broke up several times, always in an LDR. Their last and most memorable LDR period involved riding the Chinatown bus between Boston and New York to see each other every weekend. The LDR ended when Josh moved to Boston to be with Marina. Marina has just completed a Master's in health sciences, and Josh works in the IT industry in sales.

Jack and Lisa

Jack, now in his fifties, has had three LDRs, each lasting from three to four years. When we spoke, he was engaged (and by this time he is married for the first time) to the love of his life, Lisa, in her forties, with whom he shared his fourth and last LDR before she moved to join him. They have since relocated to Philadelphia together. Jack spoke to me about all four LDRs. Jack and Lisa are mediators and marriage counselors.

Christine and Ron

Christine and Ron, now in their late thirties, were high-school sweethearts in Illinois who never quite got over each other. When they finally hooked up again, she was working in Kentucky as a Youth Minister and he was getting a post-graduate engineering degree in Iowa. They had an LDR for 18 months before getting married and moving to Virginia together immediately after. Now, they have young children, and many years of a happy marriage under their belts.

Makoto and Chie

Makoto, in his forties, works in the United States. He signed up for a Japanese matchmaking service, where he met his future wife, Chie, in her thirties. They had an LDR for a year before Chie moved to the United States. When she got pregnant, they decided she should return to her family in Japan until their child was born, marking their second LDR period. Now, Makoto and Chie live together in the United States. Chie speaks English remarkably well: well enough to tell me that of two-and-a-half years of being together, she and Makoto have lived together only five months!

Kathy and Tim

Kathy has been in the hotel industry since her twenties. She was approaching forty, and posted in Sydney, Australia, when she met Tim, divorced and in his forties, during a visit to Indiana to see her family. Next thing she knew, she and Tim were swapping e-mails and working visits into her business trips to the United States. Kathy still works for the same hotel conglomerate, but now she works out of Indiana. She's married to Tim and they plan to have a baby.

Ariana and Claudio

Ariana, an American, has an LDR with her husband, Claudio, an Italian: She works in Milan, at an American school, during the week, and drives home to Lucca on weekends. She is in her forties, and her husband, in his fifties. Her son from a previous marriage attends college in the

United States, and sometimes visits, shuttling between the two cities with his mother. "He thinks we are *mad*," says Ariana.

Joan and Mike

Joan and Mike are both in their late thirties. Joan grew up in a military family, as did Mike. When they met in college, they had both signed up, and "owed the army." Since getting married, they have had several LDR periods through relocations, appointments, and deployments. They now have three young daughters, the youngest of whom is just six. When Joan and I spoke, Mike had been deployed in Afghanistan for a year, and was expected home in a week.

Joe and Liz

Joe works in the Navy, and his wife, Liz, has a full-time civilian job. They are both in their early forties, and this is a second marriage for each. Their LDR spans deployment periods, when Joe was sailing abroad, and active-duty periods when Joe's ship was patrolling U.S. shores. His last deployment was right after 9/11, and the first time Liz got really worried for his safety. Now, Joe has a shore posting for a few years.

Veronica and Steve

Steve is a Ph.D. who teaches at a military university, and his wife, Veronica, works as managing editor at a magazine. They are both in their late thirties, and have two children. Over 13 years of Steve's military career, they have relocated several times, most memorably to Virginia, which they loved, and Washington, D.C., which they adjusted to. They have separated several times as well. When I spoke to Veronica, they were expecting to relocate again in a month.

Seetha and Dave

Finally, we come to my own seven-year LDR. Dave and I met as graduate students in the same university in Colorado. Our LDR began when I moved to Indiana for my Ph.D. Dave, meanwhile, graduated and found a job as a research and development scientist in Colorado. Our LDR persisted because I was unable to get a tenure-track professor job in Colorado after my own Ph.D., and Dave was unable to find openings matching his skills in Pennsylvania, where I *did* get a professor job. Dave and I now live together in Colorado: I've taken a year's leave—maybe two, maybe more—from my job. We have decided that if we move, it will be together.

The Least You Need to Know

◆ Over three million couples in the United States are in long-distance relationships, and they exist all over the world as well.

◆ New kinds of long-distance relationships emerge when couples have prior commitments to dual careers, find themselves transferred to a new location for work, meet people while traveling or online, decide that one partner wants to get back in the workforce after several years of marriage, or have jobs that require more travel than expected.

◆ Long-distance relationships occur at all ages and stages of life, among all nationalities, and across international boundaries.

Chapter 2

Are You Weird for Trying It?

In This Chapter

- ◆ Traditional LDR models versus new situations
- ◆ How changes in the economy have made LDRs more common
- ◆ Reasonable stage-of-life considerations for giving it a shot

If you're in a long-distance relationship you're probably having an interesting experience, to say the least. But you're not alone. There was a reason this experience came to you: a combination of personal choices and social and economic circumstances that may have surprised you when an LDR became a natural choice. In this chapter, we'll see how LDRs are a trend, rather than an aberration. After you've realized that you're not weird for being in an LDR, we'll look at some stage-of-life factors that make an LDR a reasonable choice.

Do We Have a Road Map?

As one half of an LDR couple, you might feel that there's no road map for what you are doing. To some extent, it's true: you might be taking your LDR in uncommon new directions. However, LDRs are nothing new, and they exist along a spectrum. There are traditional LDRs that people are used to, newer ones that raise more eyebrows, and others in between. Once you see that LDRs are not that unusual, it will be easier to stop subscribing to the view that something's wrong with this picture. At the same time, you'll see why people around you might continue to think it strange, at least for a while.

Traditional-Family LDRs

Some professions have quietly and unobtrusively required LDRs for decades or centuries. People in these LDRs have children, travel, manage on their own, etc., but no one sits up, exclaims, and remarks on them. If you're in such a profession, you might be a military person, a merchant marine, a trucker, an airline pilot, a coal miner, a construction worker, a professional athlete, a traveling salesmen, or a business executive. I probably haven't mentioned all the professions that belong on the list, but you get the idea.

These LDRs don't raise eyebrows for three reasons: the family structures in which they occur have historically been traditional, with the man being breadwinner and woman being homemaker; the professions have been around for a long time, and are ingrained into the fabric of our expectations; finally, the jobs themselves require travel.

 Survival Kit _____

Nowadays, women can be found in all the professions that traditionally and historically require LDRs, like the military, trucking, athletics, sales, construction, and so on. Such role-reversal LDRs may cause more notice than traditional ones, but because the professions have been around a long time and have always required travel, these LDRs continue to be respected, and seldom invite negative judgment or comment.

Dual-Career LDRs

If the woman in the family seeks a career, it's the next degree along the LDR spectrum. Working women are nothing new anymore. So if a man has a job that requires travel and his female partner works a day job and is passionate about a career, well, that's just how society and the economy are changing—families are less hierarchical and more egalitarian.

If the situation were reversed—the man works a day job and looks after the kids, and the *woman* travels for work—you might start seeing raised eyebrows. The questions about your situation, how you manage, etc., can begin, with the questioner perhaps oblivious that the role reversal is the only thing prompting the question. So here, you can tell, it is getting into territory outside the social comfort zone. The family model has changed a bit more, with the woman adopting a role as wanderer that was traditionally reserved for men.

Begin as LDR, Continue as LDR

You met the love of your life while traveling or online, started a serious relationship, and he or she is not moving to join you? People might not understand why such relationships should persist when there are so many nice girls or boys around you; such a large pool to choose from, and you go and fall for someone far away. There's something wrong with this picture.

The reason such relationships remain LDRs is, of course, that the model of the relationship is egalitarian. Neither partner feels right pressuring the other to give up a career and move for the relationship. They understand and respect each other's work. However, if you are in this kind of LDR, it could be a bit of overload even for like-minded people who have never faced your situation, and it's definitely a challenge for more traditional couples, who give precedence to the man's career.

Dual-Career Married LDRs

Finally, there's the LDR that's just ahead of the social curve of acceptance: it's the LDR in which you and your partner actually *were* together, got married, and accepted jobs that pulled you far apart. Mutter, mutter.

It's social change overload: a committed marriage of equals, regular jobs in *different places*, and the jobs themselves perhaps highly specialized.

Economy and Technology

The fact that more women today have careers is not the sole reason for LDRs. There have been massive changes in the economy that make LDRs more common. First, more specialization has become the norm rather than the exception. As a result, your education might make you an extremely good fit for a smaller range of jobs than if you were a generalist, and you might find there are fewer choices about where to work.

Second, large companies, spanning countries and continents, have become more common. As a result, you might relocate as you climb the corporate ladder when your company transfers you from place to place. Third, layoffs and high turnover is common these days as the economy responds to a downturn. So people might only find temporary jobs, and move to different locations to look for new work. For all these reasons, couples find themselves geographically separated, and charting new territory in LDRs more than was common before.

Survival Kit _____

Obviously, some LDRs have more social acceptance than others. The point is, you're part of a trend. Wherever you are along the spectrum, being in an LDR is challenging. But you're not forging ahead without any precedent whatsoever. Others have gone before you. You're not weird for being in an LDR (that is, you're not weird *bad*; you're just weird *interesting*).

Stage-of-Life Considerations

Finally, some reasonable stage-of-life considerations might make you willing to give the LDR a go. Let's look at some of them.

On the Brink of Great Things

If you've invested a lot of time preparing for a certain career, say, with a graduate degree, perhaps financed by student loans, etc., you're probably eager to give yourself a chance in this career. Your partner could be in the same position. You may both, in other words, have fledgling careers, or, perhaps, careers with great things in store, which you're eager to explore. You do not want to rule out the possibility that in just a couple of years, you will have expanded the options available to you and be able to live together.

More importantly, you don't want to turn away from opportunities that you may later regret foregoing. Nothing is quite as bitter as a lost opportunity, passed over for fear that taking it would do some vague, half-suspected harm to your relationship. When your careers are on the rise, the probability that your relationship can withstand an LDR is greater than the probability that it will survive bitter regrets over stifled potential and what might have been. You might not want to rule out an LDR by prematurely deciding that it is not a good idea. If the choice is between an LDR and regretting missed opportunities later, the LDR can make a lot of sense.

The Desire to Be a Good Feminist

Women who have earned careers for themselves sometimes feel an obligation, both to themselves and to women everywhere, to stay in them, especially during the most productive years of life, and perform well. If this is you, you might suck up the personal cost of being in an LDR. If I chuck this to go back to a man or a relationship, you think, it will only encourage negative stereotypes for professional women and make me feel disappointed in myself. A supportive partner might strengthen you in your resolve to stay in your career despite the LDR. You might also have female colleagues who, though not having LDR experiences of their own, still encourage your efforts to navigate yours without compromising your opportunities.

We're Strong, We Can Take It

You might have several years of marriage under your belt: years of devoted, loving family life. Now, you might feel that your relationship is strong enough to withstand an LDR, which presents itself as the only way to take advantage of certain opportunities that you want. You can even regard it as an adventure in your later years—something that presents you with an exciting challenge that you know you have the tools to master because you are strong, both in your marriage and as a person who's seen a lot of life.

The Assumption Behind It All

LDR experts have pointed out that LDRs arise because the demands of work are, well, the demands of work. They are non-negotiable: deadlines and timetables have to be met, projects or missions completed, classes taught, papers written, and so on. The demands of professional life are in a sense ultimatums. In the face of these demands, we notice that family life is flexible and resilient, and so we are relieved to meet the demands of work by leaning on the strength and flexibility of personal relationships. The LDR is just a reflection of this dynamic. We'll return to this theme in the last two chapters.

The Least You Need to Know

◆ You are not weird for being in an LDR; your relationship occurs along a spectrum of LDRs, many of which have existed quietly for hundreds of years.

◆ There are several economic reasons why couples may find themselves geographically separated and charting new territory in LDRs.

◆ There are reasonable stage-of-life considerations that feature in the acceptance of an LDR.

Part 2

For Better and for Worse

Obviously, an LDR has ups and downs like any other relationship. The ups can be quite romantic and blissful. It's one of the perks. The downs involve making lots of transitions between being apart and being together. Here, I'll show you how you can get to know the real person through the fantasylike reunions and phone conversations so that you get closer over time, and how to have gentle transitions as you part and come together.

If you worry about fidelity in your LDR, you'll find reassurance and advice here. If you have kids, or if you are in a military LDR, I have things to tell you about how to meet your challenges, as well. Finally, we'll watch your LDR as it matures over time, and understand how best to think about it and take care of each other.

Chapter 3

Goodbye, Till the Next Time

In This Chapter

- Emotional responses to parting
- How separations generally affect men versus women
- Saying goodbye after a long visit
- What to do after the goodbye
- Being sad is not bad

Goodbyes are those sharp turns in the LDR journey that have you careening between honeymoonlike bliss and feverish (or despondent) workaholism. Or maybe you careen between co-parenting and "single" parenting. Or maybe you careen between a satisfying romantic life and a full life apart from your partner. Or maybe you careen between a satisfying romantic life and a *lonely* life apart from your partner. Or maybe you don't careen at all, in which case, give me a call and tell me your secret.

Ariana, who commutes between Lucca and Milan (in Italy), describes her transitions eloquently: "I am constantly in a state of coming and going. I am always packing. My mind is in a steady state of alert to remember things: lipstick, boots, black stockings, cell phone, journal, novel. I am in a state, always, of being unfinished. I leave ghost prints of myself and it is like being in a constant state of abandonment." She has put into words the feelings of many busy partners in LDRs. Here, I'll first touch on features of separation, and then move to parting after a long visit (short visits are dealt with in Chapter 4). Throughout, I'll discuss ways to make goodbyes gentler.

A Brief Psych Lesson

It doesn't matter if you are a fine, rational, adult—you can still have the same emotional responses to separation as an infant or a puppy. Here is someone you love, and he or she is separating from you. Perhaps you cope with goodbyes by having a tearful scene at the airport, words of love, breathless promises, etc., all of which affirm the romance. Or perhaps you bargain, as I did, trying to prolong your time together by postponing departure. Perhaps your goodbyes take on a darker hue— you feel anger and fight about something, or feel sad and sink into mild depression. Or perhaps you simply detach and are downright emotionless. "See you soon," you say from behind the newspaper. "Don't forget the milk on your way back."

Survival Kit

Knowing when you'll see each other next makes it much easier to part now. Have your next airline tickets booked in advance, or mark your calendars with future dates if you commute by car. This gives you hope and emotional continuity in your LDR.

These examples show the different emotional stages of separation, ranging from clingy to bargaining, to angry, to depressed, to detached. Bargaining and anger are attempts to resist separation, depression comes from realizing that resistance is futile, and detachment comes when you're reconciled to separation and pull back to spare yourself debilitating emotions. There may also be gendered responses to separation, which I'll discuss next.

Losses and Gains for Men

In general, men have different responses to separation than do women. Typically, men sink into mild depression. This tends to happen regardless of whether they're the ones commuting, or the ones left behind. Why does this happen? It's because most men experience the separation as a loss, offset by few gains. You know how expectations affect your perceptions of loss and gain? Well, like it or not, most of us have expectations of a traditional family drilled into us. And in a traditional family, having a partner represents gains for men: gains of companionship, labor-division, and resource-sharing. When men suddenly find themselves separated from their partners, those things are lost.

Okay, the losses are clear, but why do I say there are few gains? Because for men, a career, earning power, and a public life aren't gains—they've always had those things. There are other gains for them: if the LDR involves dual careers, they are glad for any successes in their partners' lives, and believe the relationship is better because their partners are pursuing their dreams. But on a personal level, they still experience loss. They can feel sad and bewildered at being alone. This makes separations harder for men.

> **Go the Distance**
>
> An interesting scholarly study (yes, there is such a thing) of married LDRs can be found in the book *Commuter Marriage: A Study of Work and Family* by Naomi Gerstel and Harriet Gross (see Appendix A).

There are exceptions. Sometimes men find that the compartmentalization that an LDR allows is great. It allows them to have it all: the benefits of a single life, as well as the best parts of a relationship ("the icing," as Jack put it, "without the bready, crusty dry stuff"). In dual-career LDRs, sometimes men cannot bear it if their partners *don't* work. They find their partners more interesting because they have a life of their own, and nag them to go back to work if they become too domestic. In such situations, men are able to adjust to separations, because various other aspects of the relationship represent gains that carry more weight than the losses.

Losses and Gains for Women

Would you be surprised to learn that women, too, think their male partners have more hardship to bear than they do? Why is this? It's because new opportunities for women represent gains that help ease the loss of separation (I'll get to the losses in a moment). Women, like men, internalize expectations of a traditional family. But for women, these are expectations of domesticity, child-rearing, putting the man's career first, and dependency. Often, it involves compromising their own talent, potential, and dreams. But now society offers new, meaningful, previously unavailable opportunities to women—opportunities for new experience, new stimulation, value in the workplace, independence, and a public life. If taking up those opportunities requires an LDR, why, women are willing to give it a go. They do about the same amount of housework, so that's no loss. The loss takes the form of guilt for leaving their partners alone, and a vague sense that their partner is paying the price (in terms of unsatisfied expectations) for their development. But the losses of separation, while difficult, are offset by new opportunities gained. If your female partner doesn't seem sad enough about leaving you, that's probably why.

 Survival Kit

Nothing feels quite like abandonment than to see one lonely toothbrush where formerly there were two. Keep a spare toothbrush in your partner's space always. It's a small thing, but it can bring great comfort.

There are exceptions here, too. Many women decide early on that being with their partners and family is more important to them than going off and pursuing their own dreams. But sometimes their partners might go away for jobs, or be posted far away, and they find themselves in an LDR anyway. Women in such situations might experience more losses than gains, and have the same sorts of mild depression that most men experience on separating.

Here endeth the lesson on men, women, and parting. More explanation, as it turned out, than practical advice. But hey, understanding yourself is the first step to helping yourself. So no apologies for the theory. But let's move on.

After a Long Visit

Consider the long visit where your partner visits for several weeks, then disappears for several weeks. Around two weeks before the end of the visit, the impending separation hits home. "Oh, crap! We don't have much time left!" The instinct is to begin spending as much time as possible together. You come home early from work, and your partner foregoes any work he or she has brought to do while visiting. You cram all your unfulfilled plans into your last few days. This response—panic, followed by clearing your schedule to be with each other—has two consequences, each with its own different personal responses.

First, clearing your schedule disrupts your routine. The possible effects of disrupting your routine are (a) you could go through the last several days feeling like something's off, something's wrong—your disrupted routine tells you so—and this could make your last days together more sorrowful, rather than less; or (b) you could have a golden time with your partner, full of wine and roses—or beer and fries—and feel good. Next time, see which response is more prominent for you.

Second, clearing your schedule guarantees a boatload of piled-up work later. The possible effects of this are (a) you could get stressed out from overwork, and experience your life as a roller-coaster, feeling out of control, etc.; or (b) the increased work could help you later on, by keeping you busy and stimulated when you're apart. Next time you're saying goodbye, see which response is more prominent for you.

If you have (a) responses, i.e., you are disturbed by your disrupted routine and overwhelmed by piled-up work later, consider another way to deal with the time before separation. Don't clear your schedule before parting. Keep to your usual routine, for the most part. That way, the time until you part can feel quite normal instead of emotionally intense, and the changes to your routine after you part will be less drastic. Then, the only thing that you must adjust to after parting is filling the time you spent exclusively together.

Survival Kit

If you find separations draining, try saying goodbye in the peace of your home the previous night, instead of just before parting. See if this makes you feel better.

Your responses to parting depend on so many things—personality, work demands, the stage of your LDR, the duration of the visit, and when you'll next reunite—that your strategies for easing separation depend on your observations about yourselves. Use the preceding points as guidelines, but observe yourself and your partner to figure out what works best for the two of you.

Emotional Goodbyes (or Not)

There are two common responses in LDRs to goodbyes. Sometimes, one or both partners want to prolong their together time and postpone their parting. Or it can happen that one or both partners start to pull away from the other in anticipation of the goodbye. I'll talk about both responses, as well as some of the aftermaths of goodbyes.

Lingering Goodbyes

It's quite romantic when one partner declares, "Dammit, I'm staying. I can't leave you. I'll catch the night flight/drive all night," and crushes the other in an embrace. A bit less romantic, and perhaps a bit more needy, is when one partner entreats the other: "Don't leave yet! Must you leave? Miss this flight/start driving early tomorrow!" and crushes the other in an embrace when he or she acquiesces.

Of course, it doesn't always work out. I've done both, and been occasionally burned. I've missed my own flight, and been charged $100 for the privilege of flying stand-by. I've also entreated my partner, Dave, to miss his flight, only to find the dragon-lady at the airline counter unmoved, refusing to allow him standby, making us fork over more money for a whole new ticket. After several lingering goodbyes, we learned that last-minute changes to our travel arrangements induce rage and madness— and cost money. They reduce post-travel rest for the traveler, and the one left behind has less time to catch up after the parting. It's also awkward and stressful to be asked to stay when you're mentally prepared to leave and would really prefer it. We learned, by trial and error, that it's better to just stick to travel plans.

"Why Are You Pulling Away from Me?"

Far from lingering, one partner can sometimes detach from the other even before saying goodbye. This often baffles the other, who would perhaps be reassured by togetherness and signs of regret about parting. Detachment is a natural response to separation. It protects against debilitating pain, though the detaching partner may feel quite guilty at the hurt he or she knows is being caused to the other. As Ariana puts it, "I am abandoning Claudio every time I leave, especially if I leave earlier than planned instead of waiting until the last minute after the dinner has been finished, the dishes washed and stacked away." The detaching partner may genuinely have to attend to things, like packing. As I'll advise throughout this book, it's best to have two sets of everything to reduce packing anxieties. But packing is just one (and not the most important) reason people detach.

 Counting the Minutes

Whether you're the "lingering goodbye" type or the "detaching" type, be sensitive to how you affect your partner and adjust for it if possible. People feel vulnerable during goodbyes, so insensitivity is more likely to sting. You can avoid many a lengthy upset just by being present with your partner when you're together, or honestly explaining your state of mind.

The detaching partner may also be troubled by a sense of excitement about parting. Ariana e-mailed me these words: "I am relieved to go to Milan every Wednesday night and relieved to return to Lucca on Sundays." Is it wrong to look forward to leaving? No. First, LDRs often begin precisely because partners are fulfilling important aspects of their lives in different places. The excitement of returning to the challenges you face away from each other after getting your relationship "fix" is quite natural. Second, after the unusually intense intimacy of your reunion, you will often feel ready to become autonomous again. When you're living together, these two aspects, autonomy and intimacy, can be more integrated, but in an LDR you get megadoses of each, sequentially. You might be ready, even relieved, to move on from the one to the other.

Fussing Over Your Partner

When Ariana is about to leave, Claudio starts fussing over her. "Claudio has made a pot of soup for me to take back to Milan," she wrote in her e-mail. "'Do you have parmesan cheese?' he asks. I try to keep my voice neutral when I answer because I don't want him to know how annoyed I feel. The care packages he sends—the clean laundry folded into neat piles, the plastic containers filled with food, the sticks of rose and cinnamon perfumed incense—I should appreciate his kindness but sometimes I want to protest against his careful tending. I feel like a child being sent off to camp." Being fussed over is often lovely, especially when you're tired or sick. It helps the fusser, too, by making him or her feel necessary. But both of you have learned autonomy and independence in the LDR. The suggestion from one of you that the other is not capable can be irritating. If you fuss, make sure there's no such suggestion. Gauge each other to see if the fussing is okay.

The Aftermath of Goodbye

As I mentioned earlier, partners might feel excited and ready to return to their single lives at the end of their intense reunion. They may switch gears easily and get busy with the transition to being apart. Apart from this proactive response to parting, there are three other common responses:

♦ The nontraveling partner can feel suddenly disconnected. Everything falls into place during the visits, and things suddenly feel all wrong after the parting. If this is you, anticipate that sudden feeling of disconnection by making some plans for the time immediately after parting. That way you avoid suddenly feeling like you've lost structure and purpose.

♦ There can be sleep disruption for both partners. For the traveling partner, who may cross time zones or have a long commute, it's easy to see how sleep disruptions happen. (I'll deal with travel smarts in Chapter 12.) The same-location partner can also find sleep patterns disrupted. My partner, Dave, would find himself puttering around on the nights after I left, doing things of no consequence. He'd have a strange reluctance to get in bed. He was waiting for me, at some level beyond rational thought. To ensure you sleep properly, call each other around bedtime and say goodnight, write your bedtime down in large letters and stick it where you see it, and set your watch alarm when you plunk down for night TV, so it beeps before you get mesmerized.

> **Go the Distance**
>
> If you find your sleep patterns disrupted after reunions and partings, read *The Complete Idiot's Guide to Getting a Good Night's Sleep* (see Appendix A). It's chock-full of helpful tips on the subject.

◆ Finally, there's healthy eating. After meals with your partner, who wants to go back to eating alone? You might find yourself eating cereal, a peanut butter sandwich, unhealthy fast food, or dinner out; or, eating at odd times, whenever your stomach says, "Hey, put something here!"; or eating in front of the TV (which can make you overeat); or postponing food because you have more work now. I'll touch on food and health in Chapter 14. In the meantime, keep your meals regular when you're apart. Keep your fridge stocked with sandwich fixings, greens, and fruit. Arrange lunches with friends so you're not suddenly eating alone.

Depression × Indulgence/Time Required = Enough

I read this formula in a novel, and it seems just right. It's natural to feel sad when you're apart, but people can have a weird reaction to sadness, as though the emotion should be swept under the rug. They start hugging and patting you, and sometimes it's comforting, but sometimes it's just to make themselves feel better. Being sad is not bad. Honor the sadness that may grip you. When you've had enough, life will start looking up.

The Least You Need to Know

◆ Dramatic goodbyes, postponing parting, fights, depression, and detachment are all normal responses to separation.

◆ Men and women generally have different responses to separations.

◆ Observe yourself and your partner to figure out what strategies for easing separation work best for you.

◆ Watch out for meal and sleep disruption after parting; ensure you go to sleep at a decent hour and eat regular, healthy meals.

◆ Be sad if you feel sad; you'll come to a point where you've had enough, and life will start looking up.

Chapter 4

Reunited (Again) at Last!

In This Chapter

- ◆ Time to get reacquainted
- ◆ Living under one roof again
- ◆ Balancing work and play
- ◆ Keeping your expectations realistic
- ◆ "Let's move in together"

Ah, the long-awaited reunion, stuff of romance novels and movie magic. In an LDR, the reality is not far off. Reunions are a sweet relief, a slipping into a joyful cherished space with your partner. Couples in LDRs often say they are in constant honeymoon mode when they are together. This isn't because there are no fights. It's because when you're in an LDR, the relationship is constantly renewed by all the outside stimulation you bring into it and share with your partner. You have your separate experiences, but are eager to reconnect with your partner, and this feels just as good as when you first met, for you keep having new aspects to your life that you want to share with your partner.

In this chapter, I'll talk about reunions of the visiting kind as well as the moving-in kind, and some of the surprises they can contain for LDR couples.

A Sweet Time (with a Few Surprises)

What kinds of surprises can you expect when you first reunite? Maybe they're not surprises. Couples in LDRs are quite used to them. Still, we don't often put a name to our sentiments, and when we do, it can be surprisingly illuminating.

Hello, Stranger

After a long separation, a partner's face can blur in one's memory. "I would be terrified that I was going to walk right past him at the airport," my friend said about a former LDR partner. Your partner may also have changed—changed hair color, shaved a beard, pierced something, or grown an extra chin. You have to get used to each other's smell, look, and feel all over again.

These feelings are natural and to be expected. Don't force the familiarity. Ease the awkwardness by admitting your shyness.

Survival Kit

To ease the stranger effect, consider Jack's strategy. When you reunite, spend time telling one another all the things you appreciate about each another. You'll start connecting the memories, and soon, the disembodied phone voice with whom you were so close will merge into the body before you.

Okay, Time for Sex

And of course, there's the matter of sex. Oh, but you *must* have passionate sex during your reunions! That's what it's all about, isn't it? You must be all pent up, going without it for all those weeks. You must have so much sexual energy to discharge! Take off your clothes, and let's see what you've got.

Well, what a turn-on. Actually, it *is* a turn-on for some couples, and they have spontaneous, enjoyable sex during reunions. Travel time for them can be a time of anticipation. The LDR intensifies romance and passion. Sex is eagerly awaited, and extremely satisfying.

For others, the expectation that they must have sex during reunions and it ought to be passionate is precisely the dampening factor. Some couples have sex immediately upon reuniting, simply because both feel that they ought to be turned on by the other's presence. They're tired, but they know that if they miss the "window" they'll be furious with themselves, not to mention horny, after the visit is over. Having sex now meets an obligation to that potentially horny future self. For guys, there are also comments from other guys: "How long has it been since you've seen her? Oh, three weeks? I know what *you'll* be doing this weekend. Conjugal visit time! I wish *my* wife would go away so we could have wild sex when she returns." Given this chorus of expectation from within and without, both partners feel better after reunion sex, not just because of the sex, but also because they feel they've met some kind of social target.

Others who don't find themselves having spontaneous sex during the "window" will still have duty sex before they part because they feel they ought to feel passionate by now. If this is you, keep in mind that the stranger effect takes longer to overcome for different individuals. It might take one or both partners some time to feel safe. Also, at least one of you has traveled, and the traveler's energy level could be low. If you're both stressed and/or tired, you might just need rest. Don't buy into movie and magazine images of how things ought to be, or the expectations of friends living vicariously. The spontaneity will come when the pressure is off and you've had a chance to reacquaint yourself with the other's presence.

Sharing Space Again

Sleeping in the same bed, of course, goes a long way toward making each of you realize you are now sharing your space again. There's also more hair in the bathroom, more clothes lying about, and other small signs of cohabitation that are comforting and perhaps unsettling. There are occasional adjustments to make, and I'll talk of some of them here.

Helping the Traveler to Adjust

One Christmas, Erica was visiting Dan in Chicago. She clearly had mixed feelings about her first Christmas away from her family. She spoke wistfully of the fireplace in her home. Dan, realizing she needed something familiar to help her adjust, prepared for her visit by constructing a fake fireplace in his Chicago condo. It gave her something familiar and comforting to look at. During my visits home, my partner would prepare my favorite comfort food and have it ready on my arrival. Such small, meaningful gestures can tremendously ease the transition into being together again, for they immediately convey comfort, familiarity, and love.

Idealized Memory, Imperfect Reality

There's also the readjustment to your partner's humanity. "When you're apart, you're never really away from your partner," Dan observed. "She lives with you as a voice in your head, and you spend your day with her presence hovering around. It's really quite ideal, for you can say whatever you want, and she cannot contribute too much. And she becomes sort of the idealized partner, flaws fallen away and only the good parts remembered. But," he continued, in the same vein, "when you reunite, the idealized person in your head has to give way to the real human in front of you. I'd often find that she didn't say the same things in real life that she said in my own head." (You understand, I hope, that this Erica living in Dan's head is a figure of speech. Dan is quite sane and levelheaded.)

When you reunite, prepare to get used to one another's humanity, by which I mean the good stuff you fell in love with, as well as the habits that annoy you. They will both be there to greet you. Your LDR will be stronger for being able to handle each other's real, imperfect selves.

"Hosting" and "Guesting" in a Shared Home

Another aspect of sharing space is, well, actually sharing it. Chances are that the person who takes care of the home will become more invested in it, and an adjustment will be necessary.

My partner, Dave, and I own a home together, and I commuted. After a while, I noticed that he was acting like a host. "Sit! I'll get it for you." "You don't have to do that, I can do it," and so on. I would say, "It's no problem, it's my home, too," not at all upset, but wondering why he was acting like a host. There were two reasons. One, Dave was more invested in the home, because he took care of and managed it. When I arrived, he did indeed feel like a host, without realizing it. Second, he thought I had enough on my plate. He figured I had traveling to contend with, and the maintenance of my apartment where I worked. When I came home, he thought, I should be pampered. It was wonderful.

Still, I found comfort in doing small things around the house. I liked occasionally vacuuming, or even cleaning the cat boxes. It gave me re-assurance that I had a home somewhere, since my apartment felt more transitory. I think Dave and I understood each other about this only well into our LDR. Hosting comes naturally to the partner who has more to attend to at home, and/or wants to ease the traveling partner's life. But make sure the hosting is balanced out by allowing your return-ing partner to feel at home in whatever ways he or she needs.

Travel Advisory

If you share a home, the at-home partner will gradually develop systems for bill paying, cleaning, laundry, grocery shopping, and other everyday chores. If you're the traveling partner, avoid disrupting those systems during your short visits. Respect them. (If the systems don't work—bills going unpaid, home getting dirtier, kids running amok—that's different. Then, negotiate an agreement in which you pitch in.)

On long visits, the space is home to both of you. If you've had autonomy and independence for several months, you might feel impatient sharing or negotiating with your partner. But negotiation, though slower than unilateral action, is better for the relationship. So prepare yourself to share decisions. You may end up taking leadership on some things, and your partner on others, but let that happen by mutual consent, not by fiat.

Vacation Mode

Partners in LDRs often feel like they're on vacation when they're with each other. This is typical on short visits, when you may indeed have days off. But it can happen during longer visits, too. You can become triggers for each other to slip into that mode: see partner, begin vacation. This can go on indefinitely, inducing you to defer work, neglect others, and be intensely insular, unless you snap out of it. For longer visits, it's healthier to establish a routine that includes work and a social life as well as togetherness, just as you would if you were living together for good.

Visits and Vacations

Short visits involve more compartmentalization of work and play. Before your partner arrives, you're in "single" mode, spending your time as you see fit, working the hours you need to finish your work, and playing when you want. Then your partner arrives, and you retreat into a golden bubble. Then your partner leaves, and you both make the transition back to single mode. Weekend visits involve certain special features that I'll talk about.

No Routine

There is no "routine" in weekend visits. It goes completely out the window. You're clearing your schedule, and that's that.

As Ron (of Ron and Christine) said of the weekend visit: "It's pretty unnatural. You spend all your time with just one person, in a way you never would in the same town. You plan to have breakfast, lunch, and dinner together, and there's constant, prolonged contact. There's absolutely no routine, so you have no sense of what your relationship would be like with everyday contact." He's got it, in a nutshell.

A word of caution: avoid letting your sleep patterns go completely awry during weekends visits, in the belief that large doses of caffeine will keep you functional. These will only have a snowball effect on the rest of your week. For more information on this, check out http://home.howstuffworks.com/caffeine4.htm. Don't put yourself in a permanent state of sleeplessness and caffeine-induced jitteriness. Go to bed at your usual time as much as possible, even during visits with your LDR partner.

 Counting the Minutes _____

If you have come to a mutual understanding with your supervisors about your LDR—say, about working longer hours on other days in return for flexibility when you're partner's in town—keep your supervisors abreast of your transitions. That way, during a weekend visit they will understand your early Friday departure and late Monday arrival, and avoid calling you in on Saturday (see Chapter 17 for details).

For certain professions, like academics and merchant marines, who come home for several months at a time, there is a loss of routine even on longer visits. However, here, the loss of routine occurs only for the returning partner, who is suddenly faced with several weeks of unstructured time. The other partner still has his or her hands full with the usual responsibilities. This situation can involve certain adjustment tensions for the returning partner, some of which are addressed later in this chapter.

Great Expectations

Because they are brief, partners sometimes approach short visits with high expectations. Such expectations may be psychologically unavoidable, but tone them down if possible. Short visits will not all be fantasies. Sometimes the weather will be bad, one of you will be grouchy, or you might feel unwell. It's best to accommodate mediocre weekend visits in your LDR just as much as fantastic ones. Include casual and unstructured time so that neither of you feels pressure to make the visit a well-orchestrated success. As your LDR matures, weekend visits will be more relaxing. You can just read, take naps together, see friends, and get more integrated into each other's lives. These things are all to the good.

Reunited on Vacation

Sometimes, LDR couples reunite on weekend getaways or take vacations together. When it comes to vacations, people in LDRs might want to choose the slow-paced variety rather than the "fun-filled" kind that has you constantly running around.

I have often seen people working their tushes off to make sure they have a good time on vacation. They pound the pavement, see the sights, read the tourist guides, and cram every day full of activity, for who knows if they will ever come to this place again? When you've been running around in an LDR, think well before you choose this type of vacation, for it can leave you more tired than when you started out. Instead, plan on your vacation being a real *vacation*, where you relax, see sights as the mood takes you, and otherwise lounge around and enjoy yourselves. There is no duty to see everything. If you never come back, so what? At least you savored every moment you were there, enjoyed what you did, and stopped and smelled the roses, so to speak. This attitude might have special appeal to the commuting partner, who craves staying still more than the noncommuting one. If you want to be together, cede to the wishes of the commuting partner in the LDR, and slow things down if necessary. Otherwise, you might find that partner weeping at the end of a vacation, from stress (of all things).

Move-Ins

In all LDRs, there's a point where you stay a while. I've covered many aspects of living together already in this chapter. In this section, I'll talk about additional elements of moving in together on a semi-permanent or permanent basis.

 Survival Kit

Jack (of Jack and Lisa) suggests having a moving-in ritual. Light a candle and sit down with your partner, pen, and paper. List what you love about your single lives, and will give up when you live together. Share your lists, and then burn them. Then list what you gain by, and will love about, living together. Share your lists, and keep them. Read them to each other on anniversaries.

Suddenly, More Possessions

Dan observed, "I relocated to join her, and suddenly her little trailer was crammed full of both of our things. I realized I was in her place, and that I couldn't just rearrange it to suit myself." Ron remarked, "Suddenly, Christine's stuff was all over *my apartment*. I kept saying that to friends, and she got mad."

Not only that, but also, as Ron pointed out, it's all common space. "The bathroom is common, the bedroom is common, even the bedroom closet is shared now. There's no other time that you have to share all your space like that. When you have roommates, you get your own room. When your partner visits, you share, but you eventually get your space back." Exactly.

Here are a few tips to make moving in easier:

* Consider moving into new mutual shared space. This reduces territoriality and allows you to make a fresh start. Both Dan and Erica and Christine and Ron did this, and report that it worked very well.

* If you cannot move into new space, consciously prepare to share space and make room for your partner's possessions. When Lisa moved in with Jack, he moved all the furniture out of his house. When she showed up with her furniture, they redecorated their new mutual home together and sold off leftover items belonging to both of them. If you are not inclined to empty your house of furniture only to fill it again, it's still a good idea to redecorate together, if possible.

* Create a space just for your partner, and give a complete tour of the home, with every ridiculous detail you can think of. Oh, and cease to think of it or refer to it as "my home." It's shared space now.

What, You're Not Leaving?

After they moved in together, Ron and Christine had a wonderful time at first, slipping easily into vacation mode as they did during their LDR. However, after about two weeks, they both had the sentiment,

"Isn't it time for you to leave now?" As Christine described it, "It was like having a slumber party with your best friend when you're a teenager. You can be having a wonderful time, and then all of a sudden you've had your fill, and are ready for your best friend to leave. That's how I felt after two weeks." How did it hit home that they were living together now? Ron said, "One day we were watching TV, and I was ready to go to bed. I kept waiting for something, and realized I was waiting for her to finish watching TV and leave, so I could stop hosting her and go to bed. Then I thought, *Oh, you live here, don't you? It's your bedroom now. This is your house, too. If I want to go to bed, I need to go, and you'll turn the TV off and join me when you're ready.* That was how it hit me." Recognize that you might have these feelings, and they are natural and will subside with time, and as you get used to new rhythms with your partner.

What, You Work?

Another surprise for Christine and Ron was that they both had less time for each other. If one of you relocates it can be quite a surprise that your partner, after all, has other things to do besides spend all day with you. If you haven't found things to do yourself, it can be even more jarring. Anticipate the routine, and have tasks lined up for yourself to keep busy.

Before you move in with your partner, discuss every aspect of moving in that you can anticipate. Prepare yourself emotionally and practically for moving in. Get ready to share space and negotiate decisions, adjust to new schedules in which you have less time together, and slowly build a social life together.

Ease Into the New Environment

When Dan relocated to join Erica in her hometown, he initially had no job. They were to marry in two months, and wedding plans were in full swing. Erica's relatives were all around, introducing themselves and offering suggestions for where he should apply for work. He wondered if they thought he was loafing around. Dan was overwhelmed. "I *moved*," he said to me, "to be with her. I thought, isn't that enough for now? I wanted to ask people to cut me some slack." Erica understood, and put no pressure on him.

Do the same for the partner who relocates in your own LDR. A person can be overwhelmed by too many people and too many plans while adjusting to a new life with a new person in a new town, perhaps looking for a job, and in Dan's case, planning a wedding. When you move in, go slow and give yourselves time to adjust. Ease into the transition.

> **Travel Advisory**
>
> When one partner relocates to join the other, avoid a crowded schedule of family and friend introductions, or even wedding plans, right off the bat. This might overload the relocated partner. He or she will adjust better if new stimulation comes in small doses at first.

The Least You Need to Know

- Give yourselves time to reacquaint on meeting again.

- Sharing space again can be both comforting and unsettling; both you and your partner may need to make some adjustments.

- Keep your expectations in check during weekend visits.

- On vacation, it's okay to give yourself permission to skip the sights and just relax.

- Before you move in together, anticipate, discuss, and plan for as many aspects of it as possible with your partner.

Chapter 5

Let's Communicate!

In This Chapter

- ◆ What's your communication style?
- ◆ Challenges and solutions to communicating over the phone
- ◆ Putting your thoughts into written words
- ◆ Making a tape
- ◆ Communicating involves more than just words

That communication is important for relationships seems like the oldest cliché in the book. But can you imagine how important it is in an LDR? You have less time together, less body language, and less sharing of your everyday lives. You come together for intense, special time, and then go back to a daily routine your partner knows almost nothing about. Sure, LDRs can sustain romance and passion, but if you and your partner mean to share life together, you will also require good communication.

As Dan, married 30 years after a long-distance courtship and engagement put it: "The passion is only enough to get you to the point of asking, Do we have anything in common? You have to share core values, even if your habits and tastes are quite different." And you discover shared values through communication.

Here I'll discuss communication in LDRs when you're apart as well as together, verbal as well as nonverbal.

Just So We Understand Each Other

How do *you* communicate? "I'm a very sound-oriented person," said a friend of mine. He was likely to remain clueless if someone was visibly upset, as long as the person's voice remained calm. Like him and most others, you probably have an orienting sense, too. If voices and words are important, then you'll like speaking with your LDR partner. If visuals are important, then seeing your partner will be necessary. If touching is important, you'll want to visit as often as possible. If taste is important, well, you might be out of luck, for few people appreciate acquaintance through licking (though you never know). And smell is important to all of us, with a direct link to our memories and emotions. But, whatever your natural way of relating, if you're in an LDR, you sorta have to develop greater comfort with words and voices.

Survival Kit

Tell your partner what comforts you best—voice, images, or touch—and he or she can introduce more of that into your LDR.

The Importance of Words in LDRs

There are several reasons why words become more important in LDRs: when you're apart, there's no body language, your partner may be ignorant of your daily life, conflicts have to be resolved even across distance, and you don't spend as much time *doing* things together so you must connect by *talking*. The nice thing is, people in LDRs have more to talk about precisely because they're apart, having new experiences they can share with their partners.

Hey, It's a Relationship, Not a Contract!

What are the first words you utter at the beginning of your LDR? Some LDR researchers think they should be: "Let's have some ground rules!" When I put this thought to Dan, he almost rolled his eyes. "Erica and I weren't at an age when rules would have appealed to us. It would have felt awkward in the formative stage of our relationship," he said. I agree. Yet studies show that LDRs in which ground rules get discussed have a much higher rate of survival than LDRs in which they don't.

Think of it as an informal discussion of expectations. Clear the air about friends of the opposite sex, frequency of contact and travel, who's responsible for what spending, boundaries, and your understanding of the other's long-term goals (desirability and timing of children, living together, relocation, etc.). Also consider discussing whether you'll see other people, and how you'll deal with violated expectations there.

Telephone Challenges

Let's move on to communicating over the phone. During his growing years, Dan would have rich phone conversations with school friends. So his comfort level on the phone was high. Erica was quieter, and unused to chatting on the phone. Yet their LDR led to an enduring marriage. "Our relationship probably wouldn't have survived the distance if at least one of us hadn't been a good communicator," says Dan. His chattiness helped her open up. With Makoto and Chie, it was different: neither was initially comfortable on the phone. But Makoto was keen to make his LDR work. He learned to get comfortable, and became better at sharing himself over the phone. "My comfort grew with time and practice," he said. The lesson: you need at least one good communicator for a long-term phone relationship. But it's a skill that can be learned. In what follows, I'll discuss some of the challenges to telephone contact in LDRs, and then, some of the solutions.

"Be Available Now!"

It's nice when your LDR partner calls. But what if your mind is preoccupied, or you're too tired to talk? You might feel a demand to switch gears and be available for the conversation. Your partner, after all, cannot sense your mood and postpone contact. Rather, he or she learns your mood *through* contact. That demand to switch gears and converse is one challenge in an LDR.

Marina found that when she called Josh, his mind would usually be elsewhere, and he couldn't switch gears to talk to her. So she decided that it would be best to let him choose when to talk, and call her when he felt like it. "It went a lot smoother when I let him choose when we would talk," she said. You can avoid the discomfort of switching gears by setting a regular time to talk each day or each week, which allows you to be mentally prepared for the call when the time comes. Or, like Marina, you can decide that the person who has a harder time switching gears will be the one who makes the calls.

> **CAUTION**
> **Travel Advisory**
>
> Be considerate when your LDR partner is tired or already in bed, and be aware of time differences between your locations. Avoid calling late (or very early) unless you've given your partner a heads-up and you've both agreed it's okay.

Those Long Silences

Some conversations with my partner involved listening to him breathe. His energy would be spent after a long day, and he would need downtime to recharge his batteries. Right around then, my call would come. I'd talk, and he'd respond with pleasure. But when I stopped driving the conversation, he'd have nothing. I, expecting a certain amount of give and take, would get frustrated and say, "It's your turn to talk now." The silences are linked to the demand to switch gears and make conversation. If someone is tired or preoccupied, the pressure to converse can effectively silence words. Learning to be sensitive to these rhythms is one of the challenges in LDRs.

No Body Language

When you're face-to-face, you have the advantage of body language. If you're upset, you don't have to say so. Your partner can see it in your folded arms, your tense expression, and your agitation. It's the same even with good moods. These, too, are detected through usual body language—smiles, exuberance, and hugs. The absence of body language must be adjusted for in your phone conversations.

Travel Advisory

> Don't try to carry on a phone conversation while you're watching TV. It's annoying to the person at the other end. (Pressing the mute button and continuing to watch isn't the solution. It's easy to tell when someone's distracted.) If you and your partner have favorite shows, arrange not to talk at those times. As long as neither of you watches too much TV, this should work out fine.

"I Still Don't Know What Your Life Is Like"

When you're apart, you and your partner have different experiences, know different people, and are exposed to different stimulation. It's possible you can grow apart, especially if you're both embarking on some new stage of life. As Jack said of a previous LDR experience: "She didn't like who I was becoming, and I did. Ultimately, that's what precipitated our breakup. We grew in different directions, and I was no longer the person she'd fallen in love with." How do you make sure you grow together, and not apart, when you're physically apart? Compensating for the missing everyday experience—outer *and* inner—is one of the challenges of telephone contact.

Telephone Solutions

In an LDR, it's especially important to cultivate good telephone habits with your partner. Here are some thoughts on how to meet some of the phone challenges in LDRs.

Share Your Mood

Switch gears slowly. Avoid suppressing your mood and trying to be perky and perfect. Reveal yourself as you are. Say, "Oh, hi. I'm sort of frantic/jet-lagged/under deadline, but I want to talk," so that your partner can adjust. If you're not able to switch gears when your partner calls, say so. Briefly explain why, and say you'll call back. And then call back.

Articulate the Awkward

Articulating the awkward puts you both at ease when one of you cannot think of anything to say. For instance, when I'd catch my partner in sugar-free (meaning "needing food") mode, he wouldn't be functional enough to converse. But he learned to name, and convey, his state. After a pause, he'd moan, "I don't have much to say! Sorry—I'm just spacey. I need to chill out/eat dinner." Well, that was okay. Once he articulated his mood, I was able to adjust my expectations, and this in turn took the pressure off him. Often, we'd stay on the line for a bit and chat about easy things or hang up so that he could return my call when he felt better.

Incidentally, periods of silence in a conversation are normal. In fact, they are healthy. In an LDR, phone conversations are frequent enough that they will take on some of the rhythms of face-to-face conversations. There will be periods of excitement and periods of reflective exchange, periods of garrulousness and periods of small, indeed miniscule, talk. Get comfortable with these rhythms, and you will be closer to your partner for it.

Compensate for Missing Body Language

I'd sometimes find myself nodding or smiling into the telephone while my partner was talking. It would have been much smarter to replace those nonverbal cues with "Uh-huh," "I agree," or "I'm sitting here smiling away." Don't do as I did. Start offering extra cues to replace body language. For your part, when you're not sure how your partner responded to your words, ask. For instance, if your partner says, "It's fine if you can't come this weekend," he or she might intend to be unselfish, but you might wonder if he or she is glad you're not coming. Clear up the matter by asking how the words were meant.

You can also increase awareness of your partner's physicality by sharing an activity across a distance. Jack, who displayed great creativity in his LDRs, would often set up phone dates to have dinner together, take baths together, or cook meals together. If you get yourself a cordless headset, you can do these things with ease, and picture your partner sharing your activity as he or she chats with you. It can often feel like you're sharing an activity even when you're *not* physically together or even on the phone. For instance, coordinate when you take a bike ride or do a hike, or even see a movie. Just knowing that your partner's doing the same thing elsewhere feels oddly companionable.

Embrace Frequent Calling

Let me say that frequent calling is not one of those do-or-die things in an LDR. Studies show that longevity of an LDR has very little to do with how often you talk, or even how often you visit. But if you practice having a complete relationship on the phone, you *can* more intimately share your everyday lives, and keep up with how your partner is growing and changing.

Your LDR conversations can be about more than "What I did today." Share brief stories from your past and present, discuss your feelings and responses to things, *and* catch up on your daily lives. Besides making your conversations more interesting, you will also expose your core values and learn those of your partner. Christine, who has now been married for nine years to her long-distance boyfriend, Ron, says: "We talked for, oh, anywhere from a half-hour to three hours, two or three times a week." She added, "I was really conscious that I had a whole life full of other people and experiences, and then Ron, separate from all that. I didn't want the two things to be too cut off from each other." Those frequent calls helped keep them together.

Go the Distance
Consider a calling plan that charges a flat rate no matter how much you call. Most phone companies these days offer them at reasonable rates. Compare rates for long-distance and cell-phone calling plans at www.calling-plans.com.

Get in the habit of talking about everything. It keeps you connected to the other's heartbeat, and allows you and your partner to grow together, even when you're changing. Such conversations helped Marina and Josh stay close when he was going to school near Boston, and she in Colorado. "Talking with him really opened my eyes to some different ideas," said Marina. "Culturally and politically, his location was different from where I lived, and he made me aware of different perspectives on some subjects." (For LDRs that cannot include frequent calling, see the upcoming section "Tale of the Tape," which describes different ways of staying in touch.)

Cell-Phone Pros and Cons

Besides telephones, there are cell phones, of course, and almost everyone has one these days. My partner and I avoided them because we seemed fine without. We also harbored a vague sense that they would complicate our lives by consuming time finding the right plan, distracting us during our day, and adding to our bills and paperwork. It's a personal preference. A friend of mine, who moved for a job and had an LDR with his wife, decided to forego a land line altogether. Instead, he got a cell phone and kept it plugged in at home. When he felt like carrying it around with him, he did, otherwise not.

There are some definite benefits to cell phones:

♦ They allow you to call and talk briefly whenever you have a moment, and the frequent contact can brighten your day.

♦ The fact that you can call while you're engaged in different activities allows you to get a vivid picture of each other's lives when you're apart.

♦ Travel can be more easily coordinated, with easy communication about delays, missed flights, etc.

♦ With some phones, you can easily take and send photographs, allowing you and your partner to convey smiles and visuals.

In other words, cell phones can help you enrich your LDR in wonderful ways.

Here are some of the cons of using cell phones in your LDRs:

Survival Kit

If you decide to communicate with cell phones, let your partner know when it's okay to call, whether you'll always answer, and how much you'll both use them.

♦ The demand to switch mental gears increases, especially since you probably *want* to take your partner's call no matter what you're doing. This can be risky while driving, for example. (And using a cell phone while driving can get you a ticket in some states.)

- Cell phones allow you to carry arguments into your workplace, where they can affect your performance.

- They can increase your distraction level. The temptation to make/take calls is greater when you can both do it so easily.

- They make you less present in your immediate environment. This can affect your relations with people around you, and your efforts to build a full life for yourself when you're apart.

- Once you get one, it miraculously becomes a necessity.

- A cell phone can be expensive, and add to your monthly bills.

The pros might well outweigh the cons. Remember, having a cell phone does not mean you must keep it on and be available all the time. You can turn it off or leave it at home—and there are times you probably should. Consider setting ground rules about how you'll use them, so that you are both served, rather than hindered, in your functionality.

Travel Advisory

If you're still at the exploratory stage of your relationship and aren't firmly committed to each other, avoid joint cell-phone plans. You don't want to be saddled with a contract that may outlive your relationship!

Written Communication

The written word contains both promise and peril. Promise, because written communication is personal, creates records you can re-read and savor, and allows intimacy in new and surprising ways. Peril, because once you send written words, you cannot take them back. Dry and matter-of-fact words can make the receiver feel unloved. Capitalized letters can come across like shouting. Hurtful words fired off in the heat of the moment cannot be retracted. Humor can be received as mockery. Your words can convey a tone and a message that you didn't intend while writing. Certain practices help written correspondence: responding to letters when you receive them; improving your articulation skills; describing your experiences with sensory details of smell, texture, color, etc., that make them vivid; expressing your feelings for your partner; and sending photographs. If your relationship relies on the written word, learn to be natural and expressive in that medium.

Online, All the Time

E-mail is probably the single most transformative change in LDRs. For Kathy in Sydney and Tim in Indiana, it was the main mode of getting acquainted. "I would send him questions, almost like interview questions, but softer," said Kathy, "and he would answer, and send me his own questions. It did help us learn each other's perspectives, and see if we were like-minded." Develop your letter-writing abilities even in your e-mails especially if you don't talk that often.

In addition, consider using "emoticons": the :), ;), and :(, as well as other symbols. Even exclamation points, in moderation, are helpful. You might feel these make your e-mail correspondence too perky or simplistic, but the trade-off can be worth it. In e-mails, both body language and your tone of voice are missing. Only words are conveyed. Emoticons, used sparingly, can help the reader gauge the spirit of your words. They reduce the chances of gentle teasing, say, being taken as criticism, practicality coming off as coldness, etc. They can also add humor and variety to your e-mails.

E-mail is great for quick notes, too, to convey that you're thinking of someone, or to attend to practical matters. They replicate the kind of communication you would likely have during your workday even if you were living together. And they allow you to have running jokes going through your day.

Survival Kit

Poor spelling and punctuation can convey disrespect to the reader, as well as generate disrespect from the reader toward *you*—for your poor basic writing skills! Such impediments can be easily avoided simply by reading over your e-mails before you send them.

Messengers and Web Cams

Consider using an e-mail messenger to have a real-time written conversation. Some large companies like MSN, Yahoo!, and AOL offer this service. You can "instant message" even during breaks at work because it allows you to multitask while conversing. Many messenger services also offer web cams, which allow real-time face-to-face chats. There's usually a slight delay in transmission. Also, you cannot look deep into each other's eyes, because for your partner to experience eye contact, you have to be looking into the camera, not your partner's eyes. Still, web cams are nice when you need a body language fix, or to see a beloved face.

> **Go the Distance**
>
> For a description of instant messaging and web cam options that allow you to have live video-chats, go to http://home.core.com/web/technicalsupport/newuser/communicate.html. If you are a Mac user, go to the Mac store and check out iSight and iChat, at www.apple.com/ichat.

Putting Words on Paper

When was the last time you wrote a letter, on paper? It's a dying art. My friend and I were bemoaning it in e-mails to each other. But life somehow slows down and seems more gracious when you take the time to write a letter by hand. A paper letter is also nice to receive, and it's a concrete memory you can save. You can even spritz the letter with your perfume or cologne to introduce the "smell" factor I mentioned earlier into your communication. As Christine told me, "The first year that we actually lived together was very difficult. But we'd saved all our letters to each other. We'd often re-read them, and relive the romance. They reminded us why we liked each other so much."

A charming website about letter writing is www.wendy.com/letterwriting. You can peek into the letters of lovers, writers, and statesmen across the ages, find books on the subject, and discover whether letter writing is for you.

Now for an interesting factoid: Research shows that handwritten letters have an amazing positive correlation with the longevity of LDRs, as well as happiness within them. See, I told you it would be interesting. So, child of the technological age, sit up and take note (literally).

> **Counting the Minutes**
>
> Keep a stack of paper and pre-addressed, pre-stamped envelopes handy. When you have a few minutes, write a paragraph. If you're busy, make the letter ongoing for a few days. Drop it in your office or home mailbox when it's ready to go.

Add richness to your words. Write letters in different locations—in a park, library, restaurant, on a mountaintop—and use the location to trigger your words. Describe where you are, what's going on around you, and what it reminds you of, and you'll be off and running with more things you want to say. Do it right away, before you can talk yourself out of it.

Tale of the Tape

And what about those who don't have Internet and web cam access or a handy cell phone? What about visually oriented people, who go crazy without seeing their loved one, or sound-oriented people who must hear their beloved's voice?

Taping Your Voice

I read a touching story about a military dad who sent his kids a tape every week, as if he were chatting with them. He'd tell about his life, ask questions and pause while he "listened" to answers, praise achievements (which his wife kept him apprised of through letters), and say goodnight at the end. Similarly, I heard of a woman who played a tape of her partner's voice saying "Goodnight" before she went to bed. Sometimes, when you're not able to converse on the phone, a taped voice can be a lifeline. Consider making a tape for your partner. Write out what you want to say, or chat into it through your day, and send it to your partner. Ask for a tape yourself, if you'd like one.

Making a Video of Yourself

Some LDR partners work on submarines, or in jobs that keep them lonely and secluded. If your partner is a visual person, consider making a video or DVD that he or she can watch over and over until it's worn out. It would only require recruiting friends and colleagues to tape you for a day, and you could include them in it if you like. Ask for such a tape if you'd like one, too.

Enrich Your Communication

Your LDR will endure if you grow and change together, become closer over time, and share core values. It's important to connect not just through words when you're apart, but also through how you treat each other, share stillness, and play. That is, communicating well involves more than words.

Expose Your Life Honestly

In LDRs, there's a perfect opportunity to put your best foot forward. If you're a slob, you get to clean up for a partner's visit and mask your sloppiness. If you're a neat freak, you get to clean up and mask your pickiness because your partner assumes you did it for the visit. If you're a single parent, you get to arrange child care when you see your partner, masking your usual involvement with PTAs and baby spit. Putting your best foot forward is wonderful. You have romance and excitement with your partner all the time. And that's perfectly fine. But you can have the romance and excitement side by side with revealing who you really are. As Makoto put it, "I was really afraid of a scenario where she moved in with me after marriage, and said, 'You're not the person I dated. You deceived me.' So I consciously exposed myself, and didn't try to hide my flaws." (Indeed, according to Chie, he surprised her by being "so mean," evidently manufacturing new flaws in his zeal for full disclosure.) Communicate through behavior. Relax, and reveal your natural self. It builds trust and brings you closer.

Casual Companions

It's not necessary to fill all your time together with interesting and exciting activities. Instead, have downtime together. Read books, take naps, chat with friends on lazy afternoons, watch videos. Give yourselves the chance to be still. Those moments of shared stillness are precious, revealing, and likely the most intimate moments between you.

Hugs and Comfort

Some adults, even those with active sex lives, can be physically undemonstrative. In an LDR, where there are long periods of being apart, hugs and affection are sorely needed when you're together. If you're not naturally affectionate, try a little hugging the next time you see your partner. Physical affection literally relaxes and comforts, so hold hands, stroke each other, and bring that warmth of contact into your time together. You communicate trust and safety when you do this. When you part, both of you will feel good about it.

A Life of the Mind

In LDRs there's sometimes a separation between intellectual life—full of the things that stimulate you—and relationship life, where you become romantic or domestic. It can be fun to have these compartments; however, your LDR will be richer if you integrate them. Share a life of the mind with your partner. It creates interests that enrich your communication, helps you to come closer in core values, and builds friendship. See what kinds of reading materials you keep around the house. If none of them tickle your mind, here are some suggestions: *The Screwtape Letters* by C. S. Lewis; *Guns, Germs and Steel* by Jared Diamond; *Dominion* by Matthew Scully; and *The Emperor of Scent* by Chandler Burr. Exploring new intellectual ground with your partner can go hand in hand with baby talk and chit chat about nothing much at all.

Do Be Silly

Many couples have their private language of baby talk and silliness. You probably wouldn't indulge in it in public, for people would just smile thinly and wait for you to move on. But your light, fun-loving side can only enrich your LDR, so why not show it in your phone conversations, e-mails, and letters to your partner? Silliness alleviates stress, makes you laugh, keeps you affectionate, encourages your imagination, fills what would become long silences, and reinforces bonds. It's not scientifically proven, but when they start funding the important stuff, the research will bear me out. Keep your silly side alive, and encourage it in your partner.

I don't happen to know the private silliness of other couples, but Dave and I have a full lexicon of made-up words and unique endearments, which we lapse into whenever there is a lull in the conversation. It can keep us going for several minutes, until the next topic of conversation strikes us. Some people say "honey," and "dear," to address each other, but I have to say, these pale in comparison to what's available when one allows oneself to get silly and babble a bit. 'Nuff said, or I will lose my gravitas. The point is, don't be afraid of letting your hair down and being absurd with your partner, even during long-distance communication.

The Least You Need to Know

♦ Identify your preferred communication style—whether you are visual, tactile, or auditory—and emphasize more of that in your long-distance communication.

♦ Compensate for missing body language when talking on the phone by supplying extra verbal cues to replace smiles, show indications that you're listening, and reveal your mood.

♦ Old-fashioned letter-writing is a proven aid in LDRs, so consider adopting the practice of writing longhand letters.

♦ For long-distance partners without access to the internet or frequent calling, an occasional videotape or audio tape is a lifeline to keep you close when you're apart.

♦ When you're together, avoid the temptation to present a perfect image for the duration of your visit; reveal what your days are really like, and what your personality is really like.

Chapter 6

Fighting Well

In This Chapter

- The importance of resolving conflicts in LDRs
- How to keep phone fights from getting ugly
- Navigating through conflict and coming out okay
- Choosing your words carefully
- If you never fight

Ever put off dealing with something that bothers you in your LDR? So have I. It's so easy—one of you just *goes away*. Then, while you're apart your partner's good qualities stand out in your mind, halo-like, so the thing that bothered you diminishes. Then you see each other and it bothers you again and you think, "Why spoil the visit? We'll be parting soon." And so on. Thus, the bothersome thing gets postponed till such a time as it can *really* bug you: when you live together for good.

The very fact that it's so easy to put off conflict in an LDR makes it doubly important to deal with it. Whatever bothers you has to be surmounted for your relationship to advance, so avoiding conflict only delays and slows down the inevitable. As I've mentioned elsewhere, LDRs have just as much chance of enduring as same-location relationships. So you can be sure that avoiding conflict will not help you stay together, and having conflict will not make you break up, unless either outcome was bound to happen anyway. Since dealing with conflict is such an important part of LDRs, I'll devote the whole chapter to this fun topic.

Phone Fights

In an LDR, you will likely have arguments over the phone. Indeed, this is normal and healthy. When Marina and Josh were first learning to get comfortable talking on the phone, Marina would sometimes deliberately bring up topics they disagreed on, just so they'd have something to talk about! However, having bad fights on the phone can lead to sleepless nights, with unresolved conflict coloring your dreams (if you get to sleep). Why are fights worse over the phone? Because you don't have the reassurance of the other's presence, which would convey that he or she is still part of your life. After a call, you can have no effect on your partner's private musings, and likewise, neither can your partner stay in your orbit. These factors make for more uncertainty when fighting. Thus, LDR couples have more reason to learn to fight well than same-location couples. Let's look at some ways to prevent a phone fight from getting ugly.

Travel Advisory

When having telephone conversations, avoid trying to persuade the other to relocate. When you cannot see your partner's response to this serious proposal, it's easy to overdo the pressure, and you could inadvertently upset your partner. Have such conversations face-to-face.

Avoid Escalation in Phone Fights

Fighting well is like lancing a boil. It's quick, painful, and you feel much better later. On the other hand, if you fear the clean pain of lancing, your boil suppurates, gets more ugly, and finally departs with a messy explosion. Don't choose the latter. Avoid needless escalation in fights.

Certain things within a fight unnecessarily escalate it. Avoid:

- Using sarcasm as a weapon

- Dismissing the other's concerns, however irrational or unfounded you think they are

- Putting on constant pressure to make big changes that affect the LDR (these should be discussed face-to-face)

- Challenging the other's memory, in order to dispute the other's argument (this turns the argument into an unwinnable contest over whose memory to trust)

- Fighting when you're already tired and/or cranky

- Creating fights over other matters when your frustration is really with being apart

Avoiding these things will help your fight end more quickly and less nastily.

Don't Hang Up!

Once, my partner, Dave, and I were quarreling on the phone. At one point, I got very frustrated at his unfair, *highly* unflattering interpretation of my behavior. I could no longer bear to hear him talk. I hung up. It was a great relief. Why, I thought, I can make him and his tiresome arguments go away just by doing this. And I don't even have to see his face. But I sat there a bit guiltily, waiting for the other shoe to fall. Sure enough, the phone rang. "Don't ever hang up on me again," Dave said, angrily. Any partner anywhere would feel the same.

Hanging up in the middle of a telephone conflict only makes things worse and lengthens the time to resolution. It may give you grim satisfaction at present, but could lose you your partner's respect in the long run. Instead of hanging up, grit your teeth and see the conflict through. Or agree to take a time-out and return to the discussion when you're calmer. Come to some kind of resolution before you hang up.

Go the Distance
In LDR phone conversations, arguments over politics and philosophy can feel like unsettling differences in core values. But the conflict may be an expression of your anger over being apart rather than the issue itself. You might have dug in your heels more than you would otherwise. When such conflicts seem irreconcilable, agree to take a time-out and continue the discussion face-to-face.

Avoid "Protecting" Your Partner

Lies—white lies or plain old lies—will explode in your face later, even if you told them to "protect" your partner. For instance, if you spend time with a friend about whom your partner feels insecure, you might be tempted to lie about or conceal the relationship. This is a bad idea. It creates a barrier between you and your partner that you must now protect, perhaps with more lies. Just tell the truth, and face any upsets that arise.

Fighting the Good Fight

"Several years ago, we made a pact never to go to bed without kissing each other goodnight," said Pam, who is in a thriving, supportive marriage with her partner. For the last several years, it has been an LDR, and the policy has carried over to saying goodnight over the phone. Obviously, the policy has worked for them. Their anger never spills over into the next day, and so their LDR is not subject to the complicating stress of prolonged, draining conflict. Learning to fight well might be a challenge for both of you, but it's worth the effort because it creates more harmony and longevity in your LDR.

Conducting yourself well in a fight fosters mutual respect, helps you learn about each other, makes your fights resolve more quickly when you do live together, helps you surmount challenges together, and builds trust that negotiation can work between you. So while you needn't embrace conflict and rush eagerly toward it, it might be wise to practice navigating it with your partner.

Sleep On It vs. Have It Out

Some people get too upset during a conflict to discuss it through. They fear they will lose the argument, or fear they might lose self-control, and that the conflict will then *really* get out of hand. So instead, they withdraw. Taking some alone time allows them to calm down, compose themselves, and think through the conflict without distraction. After some time they feel better, emerge, and tell the partner, "It's okay," meaning that the matter can be dropped.

Other people like to have conflicts out as soon as they come up. They want to talk about unpleasant things and come out on the other side. They fear that the unresolved conflict will fester and harm the relationship later, even if the other says everything is fine. After all, the partner who says everything is fine has come to a private resolution, which may or may not be acceptable or even favorable to the other partner were it out in the open, even though it appears to end the present conflict. Knowing this, some people prefer to just have the entire conflict talked through openly.

> **Counting the Minutes**
>
> If you could choose between a short, unpleasant conflict and a long-festering one with a rest period thrown in, which would you choose? I thought so. In LDRs, it is best to come to mutual resolution when conflicts occur, rather than sleep on it indefinitely. It saves time, and makes for more harmony whether you're together or apart.

I used to want to sleep on it, and Dave liked to have it out. I've seen other couples where the woman likes to have it out and the man likes to sleep on it. In all cases, myself included, the partner who likes to stew has eventually come around to the other's point of view. Having it out is just better. It helps you genuinely surmount the issue and nullify its effect. It helps you understand one another instead of leaving one or both partners hanging. As Christine put it, "You can't be lazy in an LDR the way you can face-to-face. The silent treatment is deadly over a distance, so you have to decide to rouse yourself and work through your conflicts when they happen. It takes trust that you can work through it." Finally, if you've built a track record of coming to resolution, you'll both feel better about occasional time-outs to sleep on it. But having it out requires that you articulate yourself.

Develop Skills of Articulation

I don't mean articulation as in endless analysis that leaves you gasping for electrolytes. I mean a real attempt to explain yourself so your partner understands your motives and actions.

Let's begin with the phone. When you're upset your partner cannot guess it or read your mind, and therefore cannot address what's bothering you. At the most, he or she might ask if everything's all right. To give your partner a chance to make things right, articulate what you normally convey through other means. The wonderful bonus of learning to fight on the phone is that you get much better at doing it face-to-face. Articulation skills, essential on the phone, carry over for better face-to-face fights, too. The fights blow over, and you can more quickly move along to the making-up part.

Here are some tips for articulating yourself well:

◆ Give yourself permission to talk about things that are normally difficult for you to talk about.

◆ If it helps, preempt your words with, "I feel weird saying this ..." so your partner knows to be sensitive.

◆ Know that for almost every emotion you feel, you're not alone. Others have been there, and you're not weird.

◆ Find words to describe how you interpret an issue, or why you're feeling good or bad, and give concrete details.

◆ Listen to your partner's response with the same sort of attentiveness that you'd like in return.

◆ To make sure you've understood your partner correctly, paraphrase and repeat to your partner what you think he or she said. If you've misunderstood, your partner will let you know.

◆ When you agree on something, acknowledge common ground. Indeed, emphasize it and use it to come to resolution.

◆ End the conversation on a good note, with affection.

Develop the habit of speaking when you're bothered, even when you're together and can convey it with body and behavior. This habit allows you to resolve issues quickly.

Confide Secret Resentments

During my LDR, I would travel to see Dave more than vice versa. There was good reason why I did most of the traveling. My teaching schedule gave me more flexibility with my work hours than did his nine-to-five research & development job. But I harbored a vague belief that, had our positions been reversed, he would not have traveled as much. I went around like a martyr for several years. But one day, I put words to my feelings: "Would you do the same if our positions were reversed? I don't think so!" Dave was surprised. "Of course I would!" he said. Clearly, neither of us could know for sure. We stopped discussing the matter and I let go my resentment.

Travel Advisory

Are you harboring resentments even as we speak? Resentments fester partly because we aren't attentive to them and fail to name them. You can cultivate resentments for years this way, and they will affect your behavior without you realizing it. Learn to recognize and name your resentments. These will help you know the real motives for your fights, so that you and your partner can reconcile more effectively.

Resentments are based on assumptions. Perhaps your assumptions are right, perhaps not. But if you want your resentments to dissolve rather than eat away at you, find the courage to name and articulate them.

Be Willing to Swallow Your Pride

"I'm sorry," someone says to you, humbly. Well, that's very gratifying. It's an opportunity to be charitable and magnanimous to the person who hurt your feelings, and show how one should *really* treat people.

On the other hand, it takes two to have a fight. There wouldn't have been a conflict had you not participated. No matter how exemplary your behavior, you might have helped set the stage. Perhaps there are things you could have done differently. So, when you receive an apology, be prepared to offer one in return. It's not always necessary, and, in cases of serious violation, it's not desirable. But when you've both said unpleasant things, it's gracious. It requires ceding the high ground and relinquishing the desire to be right. In other words, it requires that you swallow your pride. I know you're up to it.

I'm sure you can guess what comes next. If I'm saying it's good policy to own your role in a conflict even if you're *not* in the wrong, what about when you are? Should you grovel? Lash yourself to a tree? Eat crow? No, but do humbly apologize. Don't beat around the bush, either. Some people offer apologies of the "I'm sorry you're hurt," variety, rather than "I'm sorry I hurt you." The former is an evasion, and at some level both of you know it. A real apology of the latter kind is more mature, and will help you genuinely reconcile with your partner.

When are you in the wrong? Well, if something mean slips out of your mouth, it's a clear case. If you forgot a promise or an important occasion, it's another. If you unjustly accused your partner of something, it's a third. If you betrayed or exploited your partner in any way, it's a fourth.

Survival Kit

If you apologize to your partner, but still have unresolved hurt feelings of your own, let your partner know. Gently say, "You know, I'm hurting, too," or "It would be nice to get a 'sorry' from you, too, because both of us participated."

But sometimes it's wise to suck it up and apologize, even if the behavior that caused the conflict was unintentional on your part. Perhaps you meant well, but things went wrong. Nevertheless, your partner got upset because of your actions, and took the trouble to communicate his or her feelings. So again, be gracious, clear up the misunderstanding, regard it as a learning experience, and express your regret.

Let Minor Venting Pass

In LDRs, with all the juggling that partners do, there is frequent overload. A frequently traveling partner will certainly experience mental and physical exhaustion, or stave off both with intense discipline. Similarly, the stationary partner may have many challenges to overcome alone when the traveling partner is absent, and have a flood of venting to discharge as soon as the partner shows up. In either case, it may not take much to set off conflict, which flares up more easily under stress.

When partners have a lot on their plate, they may direct their ire at someone they trust—namely, each other. However, if you're aware that the other person is stressed or tired, just let the venting pass. It's minor venting, even if it's about important things. Don't waste your energy rising to the challenge. It's very likely that your partner will feel a bit sheepish after a good rest. So will you, if you're the one who exploded.

"You Upset Me" vs. "What's Wrong with You?"

Think of your last fight. Were there bitter accusations exchanged? When you're mad at your partner, you might want to accuse him or her of being maddening. That seems the whole point. But, if I may offer sage advice (and isn't that the whole purpose of this book?), be conscious of your words.

Own your feelings by saying "I felt overlooked," or "I experienced that as deliberate," or "I felt disrespected," rather than "You were selfish," "You did that on purpose," and "You don't respect me." People who feel attacked stop looking at the merits of the argument and just defend themselves. So don't attack your partner when you have concerns. Focus on your feelings instead. That way, you're giving your partner a chance to correct any genuine misconceptions you may have. And you're likely to get a more reflective, less defensive response. Give your partner a chance to make things right without having to eat crow.

CAUTION

Travel Advisory

Avoid raising your voice when you're in an argument. This doesn't mean you need to become deathly quiet. But avoid yelling. It's unpleasant and upsetting to be yelled at. Shouting merely complicates the issue by adding a new upset.

Beware of No Fights

If you don't argue at all, and your every meeting is unreal in its resemblance to fantasy, beware. An LDR can mask abusive or controlling tendencies more than same-location relationships. If you never fight, and your relationship seems ever-romantic, watch out for smaller signs of abuse or control. Don't blind yourself in your eagerness to make the relationship work. Alarm bells should go off if either partner:

◆ Does things for the other's "own good" without asking

◆ Violates boundaries in small ways, like making fun of the other's appearance, doing small things just to annoy, or treating the other as incapable

◆ Touches the other in ways and at times that are upsetting

◆ Tends to subtly disrespect the other's family and friends

◆ Steers the other toward dependence

Of course, if your relationship seems fairly well grounded in reality, but your partner just hates conflict and avoids the first sign of it by leaving the room or dismissing concerns with a "you worry too much," I'd advise what works for many couples: don't accept the dismissal. Follow your partner and insist on coming to a mutual understanding. Say, "We need to talk about this. Avoiding it will not make it go away." When your partner avoids all conflict, it's because he or she does not trust that you can get through it. A couple of experiences of coming to satisfactory resolution will make your partner less inclined to flee. However, getting into the habit of navigating through conflict together will require some initial persistence from you.

A general observation I've heard from many people in dating LDRs (that endured into successful marriage) is this: since you have less every-day contact and more gaps in communication in an LDR, give the LDR more time than you would a same-location relationship before you make a life-changing commitment. Take the time you need to get to know your partner, and make sure you have a few resolved conflicts under your belt. Wise words, indeed.

My, all this relationship talk can get ponderous. Let me reiterate many things from elsewhere in this book. Quit wallowing and complaining. Lighten up when you're together as well as apart. If life seems like a grim and serious business, dance. Cultivate your playfulness. Enjoy your life outside your LDR. And enjoy your partner.

The Least You Need to Know

◆ Avoid putting off a fight for fear you might spoil a visit.

◆ Discuss major changes to the LDR face-to-face.

◆ Be aware that anger over your long-distance situation can manifest in fights about other things.

◆ Articulate your motives and explain your actions.

◆ Don't flee; hang in there until the conflict is resolved and you are reconciled.

◆ A conflict-free, all-romantic LDR can mask abusive or controlling tendencies that emerge later, so watch out for signs of such tendencies.

Chapter 7

Fretting About Fidelity

In This Chapter

- Why being in an LDR doesn't merit extra infidelity worries
- Drawing boundaries with friends of the opposite sex
- What to do if one of you has been unfaithful
- How to keep your LDR faithful and committed

"They say temptation and opportunity are the greatest predictors of infidelity," someone said to me, repeating the old adage authored by the mysterious and all knowing "they." It's an alarming statement if I ever heard one, as if your partner would be unfaithful first chance he or she got, if only he or she were let out more. It would be worrisome to LDR partners if it were true. But of course, it's not. People in LDRs do not lose control at the scent of a man or woman, even if that person is attractive and constantly around, even if we are missing our partners. Circumstances do not entirely determine us, and what's more, research supports it (so there).

If you worry about infidelity in yourself or your LDR partner, you're not alone. The worry is quite common in LDR partners. I'll help you quit needlessly worrying with some comforting stats and facts. We'll also see who that "best friend" is in your partner's life, how to deal with infidelity if it does happen, and best of all, ways to seal your LDR off from such harm.

No Reason to Single Out LDRs

Even infidelity experts say that the best check is your gut, especially if you're not a naturally jealous person. Allow for a slightly increased level of jealousy because you're far away. We'll develop strategies for dealing with that in a moment. But once you've compensated for increased jealousy, if your gut tells you something is wrong, go with it. You may be picking up subconscious cues in your partner's communication that don't yet withstand conscious scrutiny. However, if your gut is *not* giving you alarm signals, there's no reason to walk around in a constant state of hyper vigilance just because LDR skeptics give you warnings about LDRs making for greater infidelity. They're wrong about that, so you can trust your partner and relax.

Just in case you were wondering: research shows that LDR couples have the same rates of fidelity and infidelity as same-location couples. No more, no less. (For details, see Greg Guldner's 10-year study on LDRs, mentioned in Appendix A.) So there's nothing inherent about your LDR situation that makes affairs more likely. You can take that one to the bank.

> **Travel Advisory**
>
> Watch out for signs that your partner is a serial long-distance lover, or has been unfaithful to previous partners. In these conditions, don't immediately assume infidelity in your LDR; but do ask for an explanation, make your expectations clear, and then reassess the relationship.

Here are the things that *do* affect fidelity, in any kind of romantic relationship. The knowledge can help you realize that infidelity is less random and circumstantial than one would imagine—something many LDR partners will find reassuring:

◆ **Family history.** Did your dad or your partner's dad have affairs? Mothers? Sweet old grandparents? If either of you has grown up in an environment where role models were unfaithful, then infidelity might not feel off limits or taboo to whoever has that history. In that case, it's advisable to set ground rules for your LDR and confess your personal histories with infidelity. But, if you and your partner have families where infidelity was verboten, then you can feel good about your own LDR, too. Neither of you is likely to respond to stresses with an affair.

♦ **Social context.** Do either of you move in circles where people have affairs or don't take commitments seriously? At work or among friends, this moral laxity guarantees that infidelity will find company, and peer pressure to stay faithful will be rather low. In that case, you might want to distance yourselves from associations that weaken your commitment to each other. But if you move among people who are nice, decent, and committed, chances are you and your partner will find social support to stay strong and committed.

♦ **Values.** Do you have theories about the human male—say, that sex is necessary, and it doesn't matter with whom, and it's a biological need? Do you have theories about infidelity—that it can be good for your relationship, that your relationship can take it, or that it will not harm anyone? Well in that case, your LDR is vulnerable. Have a little discussion with your partner and hash out your differing opinions about your beliefs on monogamy. But if you're both on the same page, with a commitment to monogamy and a belief that it's possible and desirable, then your LDR will be okay with the distance.

♦ **Boundaries.** Because men and women work together closely these days, there's more opportunity for opposite-sex friendships at work. If you're not good at boundaries-in-friendships, then your LDR can suffer great upheavals if the friendship becomes too intimate. You'll have to learn what boundaries are desirable and how to draw them. But if you're both good at friendships-with-boundaries, you can be friends while still protecting your relationship. Your LDR will be fine.

The bottom line: if you look at these factors and see something about yourself or your partner to get worried about, then discuss your worries with your partner. Come up with ground rules for your LDR and be alert, always keeping in mind that your partner is responsible for his or her own behavior, and you can only command your own. If you and your partner look reliable on all these counts, come up with ground rules anyway, because they are a good idea, and then relax. You do not have any reason to be especially worried about infidelity.

Survival Kit _____

Your best guide to what counts as infidelity is your partner. Avoid any intimacy that would make your partner feel betrayed if he or she were present to witness it. For your part, tell your partner what would reassure you of his or her continuing fidelity. By this criterion, secret emotional intimacy and oral sex will likely count as infidelity; mental fantasies and feelings of attraction will likely not.

Study your own and partner's values, friends' values, family histories, work environment, and treatment of boundaries, and you will feel more in control, and find your mind more at rest, regarding monogamy in your LDR.

What About That "Just a Friend"?

What *about* that friend? Well, just to use your same-location self as a barometer: if you and your partner were living together, and your partner had friends of the opposite sex, would you freak out? "It depends," I can hear you saying. And that makes sense. It probably depends on how close they are, what the friend looks like, whether there is chemistry, whether your partner is cagey about the friendship, and whether your relationship is vulnerable. Well, it's the same in an LDR. Whether or not you freak out depends on what that friendship is like. The differences in an LDR might be that your partner is *more likely* to have friends of the opposite sex, you might feel *more vulnerable* to those friends, and so you both have to *draw your boundaries more clearly*.

Why More Likely?

Jack puts into words what is true for many LDR partners. He noticed that many of his LDR partners had best friends of the opposite sex. "It's something you see a lot in women," he says. Jack suspects that the male best friends harbor unrequited love, although the women seem clueless or sanguine about this. Yet Jack never attempted to sabotage these friendships. "[Her friend] was doing for her many of the things she would normally have looked to from me, except that I wasn't around. I knew that the role he played in her life was a great support to her in daily life. She was a musician, moving around town with her instruments, and she leaned on the help he gave her. I let it be. When I visited, I included him more, rather than less."

Jack had friends of the opposite sex, too, for emotional reasons: "I became closer to women friends when I couldn't see my partner much. I needed that feminine energy in my life. When my partner and I moved in together, I felt less need of close female friends. Then, it was enough for me to see female friends in 'couple' settings or larger groups."

If your partner has friends of the opposite sex, think of them as providing emotional and practical support while you are away. Granted, this can be galling—these are emotional resources being diverted from you, perhaps—but in the long run it's good for your partner to offer supportive friendships to people of the opposite sex, and in turn feel supported in such friendships. When you are able to spend more time with your partner, the relationship dynamics will automatically change, as will the emphasis on friends of the opposite sex.

Feeling Vulnerable?

Of course, it's normal to feel especially vulnerable about opposite-sex friendships. Here's how Marina thought about Josh's female friends: "I'd love to say that I was never jealous or insecure about his relationship with other females. But sometimes, when we wouldn't see each other for long periods, I'd get insecure. I found myself comparing myself to his girl friends and wondering if he'd like me to be more like them. I'm not very interested in designer clothes or the latest fashion trends and most of his girl friends in NYC were. But the more often we saw each other the more reassured I was that he was in love with my quirks and the person I was. In fact, I was able to accept and appreciate his relationship with these other women and found them healthy. Honestly, the older I got and the more comfortable I was in my own skin, the easier it was."

Survival Kit _____

It's normal to feel extra jealous in an LDR. To accommodate your partner, offer extra information on your own to alleviate your partner's anxiety. In your own case, remember that jealousy is okay to feel—it's an important emotional clue for when something may be wrong—but it's not necessary or healthy to become paranoid. Ask your partner to offer you extra info to alleviate your worries. If he or she refuses or fails to do so, *then* worry.

As for my partner Dave, in Colorado, he had a female friend who had her own LDR. Dave and she would see movies and have dinner together, and neither felt any impropriety. They understood each other and got along. It was I who felt threatened at their closeness. Dave offered, with regret, to stop seeing her, but thankfully, the offer itself reassured me and helped me put the relationship into perspective. Deep inside, I knew he was fond of her and that it was an important, supportive friendship for him.

Establishing Boundaries

Partners who are aware of "the line" and careful not to cross it can have successful and fulfilling relationships with opposite-sex friends, but more importantly, these relationships need not threaten your partner or your LDR. Here are some pointers:

◆ Reassure your partner that the friendship is platonic and nonsexual, and that you would never do anything in private or public with this friend to jeopardize your LDR.

◆ Though you spend time with your friend, be careful about "date-like" activities such as dinner-and-a-movie. Your partner will justifiably feel skittish if you call late at night, and respond to the question, "What have you been up to?" with a blithe "Oh, I just went to dinner and a movie with so-and-so." If you are going to do something datelike, give your partner a heads-up, with reassurance that it's not a real date (and mean it).

◆ Avoid situations with your best friend that you would not feel comfortable talking about openly.

♦ Avoid white lies about this friend. Your partner may feel irritated if the person's name keeps cropping up in your conversation, but that is preferable to protecting your partner from knowledge of how much time you spend with this friend. If you conceal this, your partner will feel betrayed if it comes out later, or you might find yourself telling more lies to protect the one you initially told. These situations only create walls between you and your partner, so avoid them.

♦ Do not discuss issues in your relationship with your friend, nor confide in the friend more than in your partner. If you find yourself doing either, a red flag should go up in your mind and you should back off. Pick up the phone and reconnect with your partner, and return your partner to number-one priority status.

♦ Protect yourself from temptation, and your partner from worry, by introducing your friend to your partner right away, either by phone or in person. Secret relationships are bad for your LDR, and by introducing your partner and your friend you bring all relationships out into the open. Doing some things as a threesome, though it may feel a bit awkward at first, can go a long way toward alleviating insecurity.

> **Survival Kit**
> Avoid putting all your social eggs in one basket. Develop more than one supportive, reciprocal friendship, with singles of both sexes as well as couples, so that you and your partner both know you are not growing dependent on one person for all your social needs—someone who might become a "replacement"!

If Infidelity Happens

Well, now you know that infidelity is not a special torture you must anticipate simply because you are in an LDR. On the contrary, the commitment that it takes to maintain an LDR in the first place is a reassuring reminder that your relationship is strong. Further, your LDR has only as much chance as any other relationship of breaking up because of an

affair, or surviving the affair and getting past it. However, as in any relationship, affairs *can* happen in LDRs.

You May See Signs

LDR partners sometimes feel anxious that *if* their partner is having an
affair, they have less chance of finding out because of the distance. But
that's not likely in an age when Internet activity, cell phone activity,
credit card bills, etc. all leave trails. Also, among same-location couples,
a partner who doesn't want to be found out can successfully cover tracks
just as well as a distant partner. So chances of discovery or concealment
are not likely to be different in an LDR.

The best clues for LDR partners are the usual ones: changes in your
partner's pattern of activity including more conferences, more time in
the office, less availability to you
than normal, sudden new interests,
more interest in sex with you (yes,
more, not less), more interest in his
or her own appearance, or more
emotional unavailability to you. If
nothing alerts you to changes like
these, tell the green-eyed monster to
go to bed—it's probably LDR-related
vulnerability acting up.

> **Go the Distance**
>
> If you see something in your
> LDR that makes you worried
> about infidelity, one resource is
> *Not "Just Friends"* by Shirley
> Glass (see Appendix A), one
> of the most comprehensive
> studies on infidelity out there.

However, if your gut feeling is that something is wrong—if your gut feeling is that your partner is already having an affair—then figure out what
alerted you. It might be a good idea to write down the signs. When you
called, was your partner unavailable? When was that? Did someone in
your partner's circle look uncomfortable or surprised upon seeing you?
Who and when? Do you feel your partner's responses toward you
changing? How and when? Do you find your partner's new interests
alarming? Note when they started and why they alarm you.

Keep It Factual

Next, confront your partner. Ignoring the problem does not make it go
away; it makes it grow. You have to bring it out and have that messy
confrontation if your relationship is to survive.

Research suggests that it's best to keep the confrontation factual and avoid trapping your partner into a "gotcha." For instance, if you know there's an affair going on, don't ask, "Are you having an affair?" thereby inviting your partner to lie and then pouncing. Instead say, "I saw that so-and-so has been traveling with you to conferences—please tell me why you never mentioned your closeness to this person."

If possible, confront your partner face-to-face rather than over the phone. Your partner's body language is just as important as the verbal response. You can better gauge whether to trust your partner if you can see each other's bodies.

The usual responses to confrontation are denial or admission or weeping. If you face denial, do feel free to point out contradictions between what your partner is saying to you and what your own observations indicate. You and your partner must get to the point of being on the same page as to whether or not an affair happened before you can take steps to get past it.

Confess and Take the Hit

If you are the person who was unfaithful, do confess to the affair. Don't wait for your partner to suspect something, get upset, and confront you. Confess as soon as possible. If your partner does come to you with questions, avoid the temptation to respond with counteraccusations ("What's the meaning of these questions?" "I think you have a real problem with trust," "I think *you're* having the affair, since you're so paranoid," etc.) You may succeed in creating self-doubt in your partner, and you may succeed in making your partner apologize to you, but these responses much reduce the chances that your LDR will survive the crisis. The best thing you can do, if you truly want to increase chances of healing the breach of trust, is to confess.

Survival Kit

If you've been unfaithful, emotionally or physically, recently or a few years ago, during your LDR or not, confess ASAP. The affair is a wall between you and your partner that must be broken down now. Confessing the story of the affair can help you to come out stronger. Brace yourself for a mess, and confess!

Tell That Story

Once an affair has been admitted, the other partner will want to hear all about it, probably *ad nauseum*. If you're the one who strayed this may surprise and unsettle you, for you probably want nothing more than to confess and move briskly along. However, again, brace yourself and give the details. Your partner has a deep need to understand why the affair developed, how it developed, and the details of the attraction of that situation.

Infidelity research suggests that one of the more relevant questions in helping to understand why it occurred is "What did you like about *yourself* in that other situation?" and telling all the intimate, even if hurtful, details, that the betrayed partner wants to know. The knowledge helps your partner decide whether your own relationship lacks potential for fulfillment, whether future crises are likely, whether he or she can withstand this one, and indeed whether he or she can ever trust you again. Do not resist revealing what your partner asks for. The affair breaks trust. Your partner requires complete honesty from this point on in order to repair it.

Staying Faithful

Better than having an affair and confessing afterward is, of course, sealing yourselves off from the possibility of infidelity in the first place.

Do not fear blunt discussions of whether you see other people, whether kissing others is okay, whether you are exclusive, whether you'll kiss and tell, etc. It's best to make sure you have a mutual understanding about fidelity and infidelity in your LDR. Here are some things to discuss with your partner:

- ◆ Boundaries with friends of the opposite sex

- ◆ Extent of Internet intimacy with e-mail friends

- ◆ What counts, and what doesn't count, as emotional betrayal

- ◆ What counts as physical betrayal

- ◆ What info can be preemptively offered to allay jealousy

Studies have shown that a prior understanding helps the longevity of an LDR, *no matter what agreement you come to*—that is, even if your mutual understanding is that you will both see other people! The point is, a mutual understanding of your expectations, and an agreement, helps the relationship.

It's also advisable to renew your commitment when you feel distant from your partner. "I consider myself a very sexual person," said Christine. "There was a guy interested in me and there was some sexual tension between us. I was attracted," she said, "and we went out to dinner as friends. But the attraction only made me more 'intentional' toward Ron. I would remember my commitment and pull back. I was very aware of this full social life I had on one side, and Ron on the other, and I'd make sure I talked with him two or three times a week." Thus, Christine *had* feelings of attraction toward others, but responded to these feelings by consciously turning her energy toward Ron every time she felt pulled away.

Do as Christine did. You are most vulnerable to an affair when you're feeling detached from your partner. This can happen if you haven't communicated well for a long time, or if you cannot vividly recall your partner's physical presence. Keep mementos of your partner around: a favorite sweater, photographs, and letters. When you feel distant, drop everything, pick up the phone, and reconnect. Pull out your letters, re-read and remind yourself why, and how much, you like this person. Remember that your partner lives with you in your thoughts even when he or she is not physically present. Look around you and see how big a part of your life your partner really is.

The Least You Need to Know

- Distance does not increase the likelihood of infidelity; family history, personal values, values of friends and colleagues, and boundaries are more important determining factors.

- LDR partners may have close friends of the opposite sex. Expect to feel some jealousy, but also seek reassurance. The friendships are not betrayals as long as boundaries are maintained.

◆ If you suspect an affair, gather your evidence and confront your partner with the facts.

◆ If you've been unfaithful, confess and rehash the entire thing for your partner's benefit to rebuild trust.

◆ Reassure yourselves about fidelity by coming to a mutual understanding about it and renewing your commitment whenever you feel detached.

8

The Care of Children

In This Chapter

- ◆ The challenges of the LDR parent
- ◆ The role your attitude plays
- ◆ How your child benefits from an LDR
- ◆ Weekend versus long-separation parenting

Talk about no road map! If there are few guidelines for LDRs out there—barring the one you now have in your hot little hands—are there likely to be guidelines for LDR parenting? No. But take heart. Not only do people in LDRs sometimes raise kids, they also raise fine kids who grow up well adjusted. If anything, the children grow up more resourceful, intelligent, and special than you might think possible.

If you're resourceful enough to maintain an LDR, you need no guidance on child rearing. Deciding to have an LDR with kids in the picture has likely already sent you rushing to the bookstore to brush up on child psychology and induced you to bend over backward to be a good parent. So here, I'll not attempt encyclopedic information about child rearing. Instead, I'll touch on LDR-specific topics, like what to emphasize when raising LDR kids, how to think about your family, and how to maintain ties with your kids long-distance. My goal is to reassure you that the LDR situation is not some kind of special handicap that will trouble your kids during their growing years or come back to haunt your kids in later years.

New Members of Your LDR Team

LDR parents sometimes feel like single parents, since they wear several hats. They are nurturers as well as disciplinarians, flexible as well as firm, breadwinners as well as housekeepers, and so on ... you get the picture. It sounds a bit daunting, doesn't it? But LDR parents have an opportunity to make the most of the situation and reduce stress for everyone, to an extent that actually does not occur in two-parent households. The perceived adversity is actually an opportunity. You can make the situation work for you.

Getting Help Initially

But first ... what if you're pregnant and in an LDR? The scenario will sound familiar to military couples, but may also apply to some of the rest of us. If your partner has to be away during your pregnancy, what's a girl to do? Return to family to have the baby, of course. If you do not have family or close relatives with whom you can stay, or who can visit you, you will require some other support system. Close friends might be willing to fill the role. In that case, you might have to ask these friends for help, and draft a plan for your and your child's care that works for you and the friends who are helping you out. If your closest friends are far away, you might consider either visiting them during your pregnancy, or asking if one of them can visit you.

> **Survival Kit**
>
> Going home to parents for pregnancy and childbirth is common in many cultures. It has some benefits: first-class pampering from people who love you, a comforting, familiar environment, and a stress-free pregnancy, which is good for you and your child. If you are facing pregnancy and childbirth apart from your partner, consider being with your parents for the duration.

How can the other partner stay sane? Let's look at Makoto and Chie's story. When Chie got pregnant, she didn't speak English well, and felt she lacked a support system in the United States, especially with Makoto at work all day. So she went to Japan to stay with her parents through pregnancy and childbirth. Makoto stayed behind in the United States, since he had a job here. He'd planned to fly to Japan for his son's birth, but a premature delivery ensured that he missed the event. How did he stay sane for the duration of Chie's absence? "I kept myself busy. I found us a new apartment and furnished it in preparation for the baby. Also, I kept my mind occupied by learning to do something new outside of work." He took on a project to learn a new computer language. Now he is glad Chie was able to have a secure and happy pregnancy and childbirth experience with her parents.

Independent Spirits

Onward, to LDR parenting. What quality will help your child thrive in your LDR? LDR parents, including military spouses, find that teaching kids to be self-sufficient early on is extremely helpful to the whole family. It allows the LDR parents to worry less and enjoy the kids more, and it instills in children the quality of being able to handle frequent transitions, and cope with one caregiver's absence, with confidence. "My kids are *very* independent," said Joan, a military spouse (whom you'll see more of in the next chapter). Joan has three children who are 12, 10 and 6. "My 12-year-old can cook dinner, and she often baby-sits the other two," she said. "My 6-year-old showers by herself and dresses herself each morning," she continued. "They ride their bikes by themselves when they want to go to the store two miles away," she added. Joan knows that instilling such independence in children works, because she herself was raised that way for similar reasons, with much success.

Here are some ways to instill independence in your kids:

♦ Create in them a *desire* to learn new skills by telling them how it will help them achieve something they themselves want. Make them proud to be part of the family team, doing their bit; praise them when they do it well and let your commuting partner know when they are to be praised as well. Finally, "won't it be fun to show [Mom or Dad] what you can do when [she or he] comes home?" is always an inducement.

◆ When they are old enough to tell time, teach them to go to bed at a certain time and wake up at a certain time on their own.

◆ Divide up household chores between them. Write down each person's responsibilities and put them on the fridge or some other prominent place.

◆ Teach your children to do their chores without being told.

LDR parents sometimes find an unexpectedly sweet bonus to fostering virtues of self-sufficiency and confidence in their children early on: you and your children understand each other and become friends much faster.

Dealing with Others

If your partner can't be present for your child's school events, parent-teacher meetings, or after-school activities, it will soon be noticed, both by fellow parents and other kids. Guileless kids may say "Where's your mom/dad? Your parents must be divorced!" You had best encourage your children to confide such experiences to you so that you can give them specific answers.

In general, however, it's okay for your kids to say "Mom travels for work," or "Dad commutes for work." If your child is asked how often the absent parent returns home, your child can say "As often as [he or she] can. I'm proud of [Mom or Dad]. Yesterday we spoke on the phone and watched TV together" (or whatever you did).

CAUTION

Travel Advisory _____

Encourage your young children to think of one residence being the main shared home, instead of there being a "Mom's house" and "Dad's house." To your children's friends and classmates, these phrases are known mostly in the context of troubled or divorced families, and they may subject your children to unnecessary assumptions. Tell your kids to say "We'll be in Podunk this weekend, where [Mom or Dad] *works*" (not "*lives*").

Finally, avoid the tendency to regard questions as criticisms. If other parents ask about your family arrangement, give a friendly but brief answer. Keep it casual, without making it out to be a big deal. If possible, do this in front of your children, so that they can pick up your language and confidence when they themselves face similar questions.

Your Attitude

I've said elsewhere in this book that people who maintain an optimistic attitude toward their LDR are happier in it than people who complain and feel it's a bad thing. If you're a parent, however, you might feel there's more at stake than just your own happiness: there are small, vulnerable children involved. All that self-help gobbledygook is fine for you: you can talk yourself into being positive. What about them? Is it fair to them, or are they getting short shrift as you or your partner merrily go about fulfilling your dreams? The answer is, you can be confident about parenting in an LDR and remain justifiably positive about it.

Let Go of Guilt

Parents in LDRs often feel guilty about subjecting kids to their choices. After all, you know the LDR is a challenge for *you*, but at least you had a chance to agree to it. It *must* be a challenge to them, too, but they didn't even get a chance to choose it; you chose it for them.

However, the fact that you are conscious about these matters is itself reassuring. Remember, no child gets a say about which family he or she is born into, and every family has its own quirks and challenges. Just as having a two-parent household is not some magic insulation against dysfunction, having an LDR household is not some tragic invitation to it. As conscious, self-aware parents who have the children's welfare at heart, you and your partner are just as likely to raise well-adjusted kids as any other pair of sensitive, reflective parents.

If you're wondering whether you're inadvertently screwing up your kids, cease and desist. The problem is that you're using same-location couples as your standard, and possibly feeling guilty because fellow parents around you cannot reassure you that you're doing fine. What you *should* be doing is remembering that LDRs have existed in certain segments of society for ages, for example, in military families. Many of those military LDRs are *dual-career* LDRs as well. Military kids have turned out to be strong, capable, happy, smart, and well adjusted for hundreds of years. Use *them* as your standard, and know your kids can turn out well also.

Quit Striving to Be Super-Parent

Usually, a busy LDR parent does not have as much time as same-location parents to chauffeur kids around for after-school activities, attend Girl Scout meetings at 8 P.M., set up regular play dates, etc. You likely have *some* time to do these things, but cannot commit to them as much as other parents do without going completely crazy. Well, take heart. Your children's ability to manage without constant scheduling and supervision is a good thing. There is something to be said for letting them enjoy unscheduled time, and learn how to be adults by watching *you* have adult relationships and interests you wouldn't have as a super-parent. If you want to take the pulse of your kids' emotional state, watch them at play. See if they are communicating something to you through their actions that they cannot communicate through words. This can reassure you when you feel worried and let you take quick action when it's needed.

Go the Distance
For a description of, and elo- quent case against, the pressure to be a perfect parent, pick up *Perfect Madness: Motherhood in the Age of Anxiety* by Judith Warner (see Appendix A).

Being a *good* parent, rather than a super-parent, is sufficient. Be loving, teach your kids to be good and kind, reflective and resourceful, allow flowering without excessive management, encourage affection and friendships, and, above all, enjoy and take pleasure in them. Your kids will like that better, too.

Kiss Your Partner First!

LDR parents, when they reunite, sometimes take their own relationship for granted and focus all their energy on the children. They often do not get any time alone. This can make your relationship, the heart of what keeps the family together, suffer. Of course, the kids *love* seeing the returning parent and clamor for exclusive time, which they deserve. The returning parent, too, is likely eager to reunite with the children and be the center of their universe for a while. However, don't forget your relationship with your partner. Kiss your partner before you kiss the kids, and make it a point to enjoy each other. Carve out some time to be alone with each other, attention-wanting children notwithstanding. Make it clear that the marriage has not taken a backseat to other family ties.

Focus on the Benefits

Now, let's touch on some of the ways your LDR might actually result in *better* parenting than alternative models:

♦ LDR kids tend to be able to handle almost any experience that comes their way with poise. They become independent and self-sufficient quite early in life, and are able to speak up and articulate themselves early on, as well. More is expected of them, and they tend to rise to the challenges. This in turn builds their self-esteem, and instills pride in parents.

 Survival Kit

Studies of military children show that well-adjusted kids perceived parents as more alike than less adjusted kids. So if you and you partner are both good at playing both parental roles, your kids will pick up on your gender-role adaptation and likely turn out quite well adjusted.

♦ You are a role model to them for nontraditional family options. Your example makes them realize that when they themselves grow up, they, too, have options, and need not fit into any molds. As a result, LDR kids tend to be more aware of the wider world and its possibilities.

♦ LDR kids tend to be more involved and aware of their parents' careers. They may even ask after your job and want to know more about it, something kids in same-location families may not bother with! This, in turn, helps them formulate goals for their own future.

- Children in LDR families tend to be more curious, less self-absorbed, and active and responsible participants in the home.

- LDR kids' exposure to and socialization with other caretakers (baby-sitters, day-care workers, etc.) better equips them for their social lives in later years.

- People often communicate better in LDRs. If you lived together, you might not bother to communicate as often or as well—a strange paradox, but one that bodes well for LDR partners and their kids. Your LDR situation likely creates high-quality communication between you and your children.

Your LDR Rhythms and Your Kids

If you're the traveling parent, here are some ideas for how to remain an active and affectionate parent in your children's lives. I'll touch on parents who see kids regularly and what to expect with that kind of rhythm, and parents who see kids infrequently and what to expect there.

Weekend Parenting

If you are a weekend parent, it's important to form a cooperative parenting strategy with your partner, so that neither of you is undermining the other's efforts or contradicting the other in front of the kids. Get debriefed upon your return on how the kids behaved, what parental challenges your partner faced in your absence, and the decisions your partner made to meet those challenges. Be prepared to support your partner's decisions, especially in front of the kids.

You might find it works for your LDR for you to assume a disciplinarian role when you return, especially if your partner has a career and is doing all else. If you do take on this function, do not fear that you will become the bad guy. Think of it as being popular, but respected, and splitting parental functions with your partner in a supportive way.

If it's not feasible for you to discipline the kids on your weekend visits—perhaps because they turn into model children on your arrival—you might adopt a supportive and cheerleading role. Avoid putting your feet up and expecting to be waited on, as if the king or queen has returned home. This subverts your partner's role as the main authority for the kids. Also, avoid letting your kids play you off against each other, as kids are wont to do at a certain age. If kids ask your permission for something, ask, "Have you approached [Mom or Dad] about this already? What did [she or he] say?" There is a bonus to letting your partner continue as big boss: you can simply enjoy your children on visits. The point is to cooperate as parents so that there is consistency in your parenting.

Parenting Over Long Separations

If work takes you away for long periods, keep in touch with your kids in all the ways mentioned in Chapter 5 on communication, and Chapter 9 on military families (some features common to civilian and military LDRs are covered there; also suggestions on reunions and greeting kids). Keep the following points in mind:

Travel Advisory

It is good for children to visit the traveling parent's home-away-from-home. It helps them visualize the absent parent and feel they know something about how the parent lives when you're apart. However, beware of shuttling children back and forth too often. It can be exhausting for them.

◆ Before you leave, get out a map and calendar. Show the kids where you are going, and mark the expected dates of your next several reunions, or at least the next reunion. Tell your children how you'll communicate with them and how often—and keep your word.

◆ Children *love* receiving letters or cards in the mail, and once you start writing they will like the habit of writing back. Give your children pre-addressed, stamped envelopes for this purpose.

◆ Keep in touch with your child's school while you are away, so that the teachers and principal know you take an active interest and are available to be approached with concerns.

◆ Have your partner turn on a tape recorder in secret, and send you tapes of Christmases, birthdays, etc., that you have to miss.

♦ Send your children tapes of your own voice or leave behind tapes reading their favorite stories, introducing them to new ones, or simply telling about your doings and hopes for them.

♦ While you're away, create a box for each child with a treasury of items collected while you're apart, to present later: rocks, flowers, mementos from your travels, little notes to your kids, storybooks from the places you visit, and so on.

♦ Present each child with a calendar before leaving, and ask them to fill in something for each day: a line about an event, a thought he had, or something she enjoyed or disliked. When you return, the calendars will give you a sense of their days.

♦ When you reunite, *expect* to feel unnecessary for a few days. Let the kids approach you instead of rushing to embrace them. Ease the transition by seeking opportunities to be helpful, and be supportive of parenting decisions taken in your absence.

The Least You Need to Know

♦ Give your child language and confidence for the questions and assumptions he or she may face in school from peers, teachers, or other parents.

♦ Avoid guilt-induced super-parenting, which might prompt you to overschedule yourself and your children to compensate for their perceived hardships.

♦ The LDR has benefits for your kids, since they quickly learn to be adaptable, self-sufficient, articulate, curious, and capable of handling new situations.

♦ Develop a consistent, cooperative parenting strategy with your partner so that the intermittent parent does not end up undermining or contradicting the main caregiver during visits.

9

Homeland Security for the Military Couple

In This Chapter

- ◆ Putting your affairs in order before deployment
- ◆ Coping while your partner is away
- ◆ Homecoming issues
- ◆ Changes in your partner
- ◆ Domestic abuse

New military couples have some quick growing up to do. The relationship may be quite young when it's faced with the challenges of deployment, and those challenges are intensified by a "right stuff" culture that eschews admissions of weakness. No, really? Yes. As Joan, a wise military wife of 15 years, explained very sweetly, "The military is not a place for sissies, you know. I have compassion for new couples because I've been in their shoes; but I wish they would do more to help themselves. Some weep constantly, and their children watch them, take their cues from them, and keep weeping too!"

On the plus side: in the military, unlike among civilians, an LDR is *normal*. As Veronica, a military spouse of 13 years, told me, "For military couples, separations are the way life is. We have to adopt a proactive approach, or else we'd be experiencing separations as constant loss." A family-ready infrastructure exists for the sole purpose of supporting you, your partner, and your kids. The military understands you; they've found that happy families make for less attrition, so they constantly invest in research to understand the psychology of you. If you think your emotions and experiences are far too weird to qualify for understanding, banish the thought. The people around you might be giving you "tough love," but you can find the support and resources you need in the military. From relief at seeing your spouse leave, to emotional challenges while he or she is away, to financial challenges, your experiences and responses are understandable. The military has created outreach that can show you you're not alone and give you a boost—if you only give it a chance.

In this chapter, I'll discuss some concerns special to military LDR couples and ways to allay those concerns so that your military LDR becomes strong and resilient.

When the Orders Come

You might be in an LDR even before deployment—away for a week or two, back for a bit, then off again. You navigate the same transitions most other LDR couples do. But when deployment orders come, you shift into a different gear. "A few years ago, I was scheduled to be deployed in January 2002," said Joe, who serves in the navy. "After 9/11, my deployment orders came early—five months before my scheduled date, in fact. We were expecting it," he added, "but it was the first time my wife, Liz, was genuinely worried for my safety." With an active war going on, many military couples face precisely the same worries as Liz, so let's discuss some predeployment practices that can ease this transition.

Know What to Expect: Responses to Separation

You might find your mind abuzz with all the practical things that require your attention. You could also experience some strange emotions. You might weep at the turn of events, or find yourself becoming more clingy or fearful, even as your partner becomes distant. You may find yourself picking fights, getting depressed—or not feeling much of anything, and indeed quite detached from your partner. Some deployment anxieties can even manifest in physical symptoms like headache, diarrhea, loss of appetite, and sleeplessness. As described in Chapter 3, these are responses to separation, and the accompanying feelings of loss of control. They may be more intense before deployment because of worries for the deployed partner's safety.

> **Go the Distance**
>
> A helpful guide for all military families preparing for deployment can be found at the Air Force website at www.afcrossroads.com/ famseparation/predeployment_ menu.cfm.

Understanding your responses can help buffer them. Joe told me, "I have young people coming to me saying, 'She's getting on me about things that don't normally bother her. She keeps saying clean this, do that. I don't get it. I'm leaving soon, and we're fighting more than ever.' Well," continued Joe proudly, "I explain to them that it's separation anxiety. Knowing why it's happening helps them, you know, ride it a little better." Exactly. Recognizing your state can help you be the driver of these emotions, instead of being driven by them. It can also help you understand and handle separation anxiety in others.

The deployed partner might suddenly become all business. There might be a puzzling withdrawal of emotional energy from you. Worst of all, he or she might display an ill-concealed and unflattering eagerness to leave you. Why? As one soldier told me, "You can feel like you've been practicing to be on a team, but so far have been sitting on the bench. So getting your orders finally gives you chance to get active." The deployed partner likely feels a mixture of intimidation and eagerness, but whatever the emotion, you might feel like your partner's not 100 percent with you.

> **Survival Kit**
>
> Studies have shown that new couples have a more challenging time reintegrating after a separation, while older military couples manage better. If you're a new couple, take steps now to lay the groundwork for successful reintegration by making a financial plan, creating a support system, and discussing ground rules.

Finally, if you are a new couple, you might have tremendous insecurities about your relationship. These worries are not to be minimized. In the next sections, I'll discuss how newer couples can anticipate and plan to avert some typical red flags.

Set Up a Support System

The deployed partner will go to a deployment briefing, where he or she receives contact information, instructions, Family Support Group (FSG) information, and requests for your own contact information. *Gathering and providing the requisite info at this stage is important.* Why? Because once the deployed partner is gone, these bits of paper are a lifeline for the partner left behind. So though your mind may be all over the place, give correct and detailed information to your commanding officer and share the requisite detailed information with your partner, especially about the FSG and its services.

Introduce your spouse to as many of your colleagues as possible. If you're in the National Guard or Reserves, you might not have shared much about the military aspects of your life with your partner. Well, you will soon be gone, and your partner will sorely need support during the separation; family may be far away, and civilian friends, though needed, may not be as effective as military ones. Use part of your pre-deployment preparation time to introduce your partner around to your platoon members and their partners. If your partner is not attracted by the idea of organizational support from an FSG ("official friends," so to speak), such informal introductions well before you leave can help ease your partner into the new situation.

Survival Kit _____

A new, interesting, and fun resource for military spouses comes in the form of *Military Spouse* magazine, started by—you guessed it—enterprising military spouses. Learn about it at http://militaryspousemagazine.com, where you can also subscribe, find links, and participate in discussion forums.

Make a Financial Plan

Managing money is, unfortunately, not intuitive. Both military personnel and their spouses have been known to get into deep financial holes.

Moreover, during deployment, a young left-behind spouse, with power-of-attorney over military pay, the ability to open charge cards, and little experience with having financial responsibilities, can wreak havoc on a family's finances. "Sometimes soldiers come home to see their savings wiped out," said Joan. Joe has seen people return home to find they have no home.

Make a financial plan before you leave (see Chapter 11 for suggestions): review your income, your bills and other expenses, and your debts and future needs; then hammer out how much you will spend on what, how you will repay debt and avoid racking up new debt, how you'll maintain access to your accounts, and how you'll keep track of money. It ensures your relationship's security when apart, and avoids unnecessary strains when you reunite. Even if you're taking home a monthly pay of under $2,000, your "real income" can be quite comfortable because of your housing allowance, shopping discounts, sliding-fee childcare, food stamps, health and dental, etc. In short, *you can live within your means*. Plan to do so. If you and your partner are not money-savvy, sign up for a financial management class. Online tutorials, free phone consultations, and local workshops are available to you from various sources like the Army One Source, the Army Community Service (ACS), and voluntary support groups. Contact your commanding officer or the ACS office for help signing up for financial education.

National Guard and Reserve officers typically see a smaller paycheck during deployment, less than the pay from their civilian jobs. However, under the Soldiers and Sailors Relief Act, you could get reduced interest rates on car and home loans. When you and your partner make your financial plan, take advantage of every financial break you can get.

> ### Go the Distance
>
> If you set up a free account at www.armyonesource.com, you can receive personalized financial help over the phone. Financial workshops and online resources can also be found by clicking on "Money Questions" at www.armycommunityservice.org/home.asp. Explanations of military pay systems can be found at www.silentwarriors.net/index.html.

Set Ground Rules for Fidelity

I once web-surfed my way into a discussion forum for military people. One young woman, new to military life, sought support for what sounded like a fairly traumatic situation: her fiancé had cheated on her one month after their engagement, and was due to be deployed another month later. The woman was distraught, worried sick that he'd be a "stereotypical military man," cheating on her while they were apart. She begged for advice. The response to her post? Everyone attacked her for suggesting that military men cheated. The irony? *It had happened to her!* The upshot: the novice military spouse received neither sympathy nor advice from fellow spouses, only a bunch of how-dare-you's.

I told Joe this story, and he said, "See, adultery is punishable in the military, and some navy folks consciously remove themselves from temptation. But it does happen." Joe does what he can to discourage bad behavior when his ship docks. "We have to be ambassadors," he explained, "not fit bad stereotypes. I've kept some at-risk people on board the ship. It's like a punishment." When I told Joan the story of the online thread, she said, "Oh, that's too bad." She added, "The hardest news I have to give people is that they tested positive for something— something they got from their partners." Joan, you see, is a nurse. "Left-behind spouses sometimes cheat, and deployed people sometimes cheat. It does happen. And there's more divorce."

Consider laying some ground rules with your partner. Review Chapter 7 to get on top of your concerns, *if* you have concerns. If people around you or your partner tend to tolerate infidelity, perhaps attributing it to stress, distance, loneliness, opportunity, and the need to blow off steam, it's one of the red flags mentioned in Chapter 7. However, remember: your relationship can survive even infidelity, if you commit to rebuilding trust. Also remember that thousands of military couples stay faithful and committed. So talk with your partner about fidelity concerns, negotiate ground rules, and come to an understanding. If possible, do this long before deployment orders actually arrive.

Make Arrangements at Home

Your partner will have to attend to *all* practical matters in your absence. So it's best to take a day or two to demonstrate tasks that you normally do. If you're the one who maintains the car, mows the lawn, cleans the house, pays the bills, does the laundry, cooks the food, or whatever, show what you do and explain how you do it, so that your partner is well prepared to attend to these things while you're gone. Or review your finances to see whether you can "outsource" some of these tasks to professional services for lawn care and house cleaning, and make those arrangements before you leave.

> **Counting the Minutes**
>
> If you're in the Reserves or National Guard, save yourselves the time and anxiety of trying to win your job back when you return. Ensure that you and your boss know, in advance of your leaving, about the law, USERRA, that protects your job. Learn about it at www.military.com/Resources/ ResourcesContent/ 0,13964,31004-0,00.html.

Prepare Your Children

I discussed LDR parenting in Chapter 8, so here I'll only touch on supplemental information. When you receive your deployment orders, the best strategy is to provide your children with information rather than withhold it. To children, the information is comforting. If other military families surround them, or if they just watch TV, they're going to hear about casualties anyway, so sheltering them from the nature of your job is pointless. In fact, it's better to take charge of how they get the information than to leave it to circumstances beyond your reach. When your deployment orders come:

◆ Get out a map and show your kids where you'll be going. Read up together on the culture and language of the place.

◆ Tell your kids the *reason* you're going there, what you'll be doing, who you'll be with, and all the precautions that will keep you as safe as possible.

◆ Express your own feelings, good and bad, about the deployment, and let your kids do the same.

◆ Get out a calendar and tell your children when you'll likely come back. Time is a difficult concept for young children to grasp, but telling them to cross off the days on the calendar can help them.

◆ Assure your kids about how, and how often, you'll communicate with them.

These practices can create security for your children while you are away.

Saying Goodbye

Finally, keep in mind that a deployment goodbye can be quite awkward. Nothing profound need come to mind, and you might be filled with mundane chatter when the time finally comes. You might even wish to cry, and wonder why you cannot. But don't worry: your partner knows of your love. He or she will be reassured by a warm hug and an "I love you. Please take care of yourself." You could also write a note to your partner and hide it in a place where he or she will find it later, full of all the loving things you want to say. Refer to Chapter 3 for what to expect after saying goodbye and easing the transition.

During Deployment

While your partner's away, will things get easier or more difficult? It can depend on the maturity of your relationship. When you're just starting out, it can be quite tough. But if you're used to military rhythms, and you and your partner have many years behind you, things can actually get easier while your partner is away.

Going Home to Parents

Some young spouses, facing a void after their partner leaves, perhaps with a young child to care for, go home to their parents. If this is you, here are some pros and cons of the decision.

The pros:

◆ It may save you money on rent and other expenses, an important factor for young, financially strapped couples.

♦ You have loving emotional comfort when you're apart and practical support for child rearing.

♦ Your child will be close to his or her grandparents, always a good thing.

♦ You have a worry-free situation, which buys you time to think, plan, educate yourself, organize, and adjust.

The cons:

♦ It is a temporary solution, one that postpones your transition to independence.

♦ It prevents the development of a support network among military spouses that would provide you more long-term ability to thrive during separation.

♦ It might affect your ability to reintegrate well when your partner returns, since you have returned to being "daughter" or "son," rather than "wife and mother" or "husband and father" in your partner's absence.

If you do go to your parents' home in your partner's absence, use the time to develop your skills—financial, parenting, and professional—so you can be independent the next time around. You might also stay in touch with the FSG network so that you can continue your acquaintance with its members after your spouse returns. Finally, move back into the home you will share with your partner several weeks before he or she is due to return, so that you can mentally and physically prepare for your life together.

Keep Track of Spending

One soldier came home to find the family $10,000 in debt. He was astounded. "What did you spend it on?" he asked his new wife. "It was all for things we needed," she explained. They had relocated just before his deployment, and she had furnished and decorated the home in his absence. "Do you have any records? Can I see them?" he asked. She didn't. That was rough. But, "she's the love of my life," the soldier told me. "Unconditional love got us through that bad patch." Several years later, the marriage is thriving and happy—but the couple has separate bank accounts. They had to pay off the $10,000 debt, of course. Financial strains can hurt a marriage. Avoid testing your partnership this way; you're tested in enough other ways already.

Live within your means and keep track of your spending. Write everything down and keep receipts in a box. Take a military financial management class, as mentioned earlier. And as suggested in Chapter 11, install and learn to use money software on your computer; it makes keeping track easier.

Living Among Civilians

You may be surprised to hear that civilians often do not know their neighbors. Maybe it's because front porches have disappeared; maybe we're more paranoid about safety and privacy; maybe we're busier; who knows? Joe, who lives among civilians, realized the difference early on. "I'd invite neighbors over for BBQs, and they'd be pleased and surprised, as if to say 'Really? You want to hang out with me?' I'd be, like, 'Sure.'" Military spouses living among civilians are often shocked at the lack of neighborly contact, and dismayed that connections seem difficult to forge. If you've lived around military families, on or off base, you've probably had a much different experience: warmer, richer, more neighborly, and more supportive. And here's the rub: about 70 percent of military families today find housing in civilian communities.

There's a plus: the quality of civilian housing is often better than housing on base. As I reiterate in Chapter 13, the quality of housing is important for LDR partners' well-being. Decent housing, whether among civilians or among other military families, does a lot for your mental health.

> **⚠ Travel Advisory**
>
> If you're living among civilians, avoid seeking refuge entirely among military folk. Avoid insularity and, as psychologists call it, "institutionalization." Regard your presence among civilians as an opportunity. Share your life and learn about theirs. It can be a rewarding and mutually enriching experience.

Clearly, living among civilians is a mixed blessing that requires an adjustment. You face the double challenge of being in an LDR, something most people don't understand anyway, *and* being a military spouse, something many civilians have no clue about (people might not, for instance, realize that "I admire you; in your shoes, I'd always be worrying that my [wife's or husband's] life was in danger," is not a good thing to say to you).

So what are you to do if you find yourself in nice housing, but among people who cannot relate to your experience? "Make contact with the leader of your Family Readiness Group," advises Joan, "and then hope and pray that he or she is a good leader who will help you make connections with other military spouses." (Note: Family Support Groups are called Family Readiness Groups in many military bases, and provide networking opportunities for spouses both on and off base.) Joe's advice: "Understand that civilians *won't get it.* When we were living among civilians, my wife was climbing the walls and went through bouts of depression." What helped her? "She got back into the workforce," said Joe. "That helped. She has a good friend at work now. The friend didn't really get military life either, but now we've set her up with a military guy, they're engaged, and she gets it," he concluded, pleased. A job will increase your duties, but it can ease financial burdens, stimulate your mind and growth, and help you adjust. Finally, if, like Veronica, you meet civilians in LDRs of their own, you can find kindred spirits there. "I had great camaraderie with civilians I knew in long-distance situations," she said. Since LDRs are be-coming more common in the civilian world, you might well find people who share, to some extent, your experience.

> **Survival Kit**
>
> If you find that there's no Family Readiness Group for your partner's unit, consider taking the initiative and starting one. Contact the unit commander to express your interest. You can get more information at www.silentwarriors.net/frg4.html and www.vtguard.com/FamilyReadiness/How%20to%20start.htm.

Keep in Touch

When you're deployed, you'll leave many important decisions to your spouse. "We really didn't want to e-mail about how we were spending money and every decision about the children," said Joe. However, you can have daily contact with your partner. You can plan to have morning coffee together while e-mailing (if you're in the same time zone, that is); you can send two or three e-mails a day; you can send letters. "Sometimes," said Joe, "I felt closer to my wife when I was far away on a ship than when we were together. I'd have just received a letter, and be thinking about her and feeling good." Why might this feeling of closeness be greater when you're apart? Because then, you make it a point to communicate; when you're together, you may not! It's one of the bonuses of an LDR. So keep in touch with your partner in ways described in Chapter 5.

Travel Advisory _____

Communicate about daily things, but be sensitive about the possible disconnect between your and your partner's daily challenges. Hearing about how it drives you crazy when your daughter leaves shampoo bottles strewn around the bathroom floor will not make for good conversation with a partner who is concerned with body armor in a war zone. When you communicate, practice switching gears more quickly, so that you can communicate about things that present comfortable daily news, rather than jarring contrasts to your partner's situation.

If you're in the National Guard or Reserves, with a civilian job you want to have securely waiting for you, keep in touch with your office as well. An occasional e-mail to bosses and co-workers, and a letter via snail mail, say, once a month, keeps you in their thoughts. It makes your life vivid to them. They like knowing what you are up to while you muck around in the world, far from your job.

Kids and the Deployed Partner

When your partner is deployed, you might wonder how much to communicate about his or her doings. "We never make a big deal about my husband while he's away," said Joan. "We don't, you know, _discuss_ him. I don't want the children getting negative, worrying, and feeling burdened." Does she protect them from information? "I don't protect the children from TV coverage of the war or anything. And if they want information, we encourage them to ask." Did her husband keep in touch with the kids? "Oh, yes," she said. "He e-mails them separately, just a couple of lines, and they write back." Clearly, the openness-with-casualness policy has worked. "My kids are very independent," said Joan. "Military kids tend to be that way."

However, be aware of signs of anxiety that may creep in. "My six-year-old told her grandma she was having dreams that her daddy had died," said Joan, "and her grandma told me about it." How did Joan handle it? Did she immediately go into damage-control mode, having a serious talk with the children? "Oh, no," said Joan, calm as milk. "When my husband came home in October for R&R, I told him about it. He re-assured the children. He said, 'I'm in a safe place,' and showed them pictures of where he worked and lived. My daughter stopped having the dreams after that."

The loss of a parent feels life-threatening to a child; so a military child with a deployed parent needs reassurance on that count. If you're not sure how to handle parenting concerns specific to your partner's deployment, go to the websites mentioned earlier or contact your FSG. You will find your answers there.

Christmas and Other Holidays

Holidays can be happy or poignant, depending on whether you get to see your partner or not. "Christmas was tough this year," said Joan. "But we have his presents waiting for him, under a small tree that we kept just for that purpose." Occasions like Father's Day or Mother's Day can be tough on children when the relevant parent is gone, so be extra-sensitive and nice to your kids on those days, and make extra time for them.

Reunions

You'll likely know the approximate date of your partner's return. When I spoke to Joan, who lives among military families, she and her kids were painting "Welcome Home" signs for her husband, who was due to return soon. "It's a busy time around here," she said. "People who went home to parents are coming back, and everyone's painting signs and getting ready." Wherever you live, there are aspects to the homecoming you'll share with other military couples. I've already touched on parenting aspects; here I'll touch on a few others.

Avoid Surprises

Sometimes, your return date might change. It might be moved forward or pushed back. So there's some uncertainty about the exact day or even week of your arrival. If you're sent home earlier than expected, you might think it would be very romantic to surprise your partner. After all, it's been done successfully—in movies. "We really don't like to be surprised," said Joan. "A husband or wife coming home after deployment is a mental adjustment, you know. You're going to be changing roles and you want to mentally prepare for that. You want to make everything nice, so you want a chance to clean up, prepare the house, make the signs, make everything presentable, and review your decisions to make sure nothing's left undone. When you get surprised, it makes the transition more challenging." Perfectly understandable, isn't it? So, deployed person, avoid surprising your partner when you return home. Give the heads-up when you yourself receive it.

> **CAUTION**
> ### Travel Advisory
> If you're returning home for a little R&R in the midst of deployment, be aware that leaving after R&R might be bittersweet. You were ready to leave the first time; this time you might not be, especially after a golden time with your family. Make the best of your time and enjoy your family fully, but brace yourself for a more poignant and wrenching goodbye.

Greeting Children

Your young kids may not actually recognize you when you return. Avoid snatching them up in your arms as they look shyly at you. They need to get reacquainted with you. "I greet them in a very friendly way, very casually," said Joe. "I don't hug or pick them up. Then, they get used to the sound of my voice and things start clicking in their minds." Joe continues his day, perhaps settling down at some point to watch television with his wife. "Well, you know how kids are. They can't stand not being at the center of things. Soon enough, they'll start climbing between us on the couch. I greet them, welcome them, and then I start holding and hugging them." In other words, Joe keeps himself approachable and friendly, and lets the children approach him when they're ready; a wise policy.

Not Your Kingdom Anymore

Every military soldier is taught about this, but the reality of it still takes some by surprise: it's not your kingdom anymore. After a certain amount of authority that you enjoy in the military, you might return with a zero-tolerance, do-it-my-way habit that's hard to break. "It can take about a year to readjust," said Joe. The assumption of total command can wear thin on your spouse who, in your absence, has likely become remarkably capable and independent, learned new skills, made decisions alone, and parented for the two of you—feats which are comparable to your own achievements during deployment.

To help yourself adjust to humility, do the following:

◆ Avoid criticizing decisions made in your absence. If you do, your spouse would be perfectly justified in snapping back with: "Well, if you'd been here, you could have done it your way, right?"

◆ Prepare to feel superfluous and unnecessary for several days. Avoid reacting to this feeling by pushing your point of view on how things should be done. You'll become necessary soon enough, and without arousing resentment, if you just give it some time.

◆ Look for opportunities to be helpful. It's the best way to ease all of you into the new situation.

◆ Show appreciation for the decisions your partner made in your absence; they were not easy to make without a sounding board, but your partner did it. Notice and praise achievements.

Flexible Spouse

Studies show that the most successful military spouses are the "androgynous" ones, meaning those who are able to adapt to changing roles. "The military has evolved a lot, by its own past standards," said Veronica, "and the dynamics have changed. There are more working women, and the norm these days is the dual-working family." Still, military couples tend to adopt traditional family roles of mother-nurturer and father-disciplinarian when the family is together. So military wives live out an interesting paradox. When apart, they are probably more independent, capable, resilient, and skilled than their civilian counterparts; in other words, they are the ultimate feminists, showing just how much women can achieve when the opportunity presents itself. However, when the husband returns, they travel a greater social distance than their civilian counterparts to now become traditional wives and mothers at home, while also having careers. It's no surprise that flexible military spouses are the most successful ones. There's much for them to be flexible about.

With flexibility in mind, prepare to start sharing authority and slowly relinquishing some of your own unilateralism. It will slow down decision-making and may make you impatient: so many questions about things that you know work quite well! But anticipate these reactions and, when you feel them rising, take a mental step back. The world will not end if your spouse gets to experiment with a different method than you yourself use. However, do feel free to request a gentle transition. Speak up if you feel trampled on or unappreciated for your efforts.

Changes in the Military Partner

Experiences during deployment might have affected your partner quite deeply. Your partner might come back changed. If he or she gets depressed and doesn't feel the same, don't panic. Your partner may be digesting and processing emotions having to do with experiences during deployment that he or she might not feel ready or ever want to talk about. It's probably a good idea, even if your partner does *not* appear changed, to give him or her three or four months of space and quiet while he or she readjusts to being back home. In time, your partner will likely gradually become more emotionally present and take joy in being back with family.

If your partner seems increasingly dysfunctional over time, you can suggest counseling. Your partner's commander can direct you to military resources for counseling, or, if you would like referrals to outside counselors, call 1-800-464-8107. The military pays for up to six free visits to such outside counselors, who treat most non-life-threatening topics as confidential. Or you could suggest speaking to a chaplain; however, here there will be more variability in the type of counseling or advice that you get.

Dealing with Domestic Violence

If your spouse shocks you by abusing you or your children, take action immediately. "We had a case of a soldier who hit his 6-year-old son," said Joan, "and he'd never done anything like it before." Joan also sees wives who tearfully confide instances of domestic violence from recently returned spouses. They remain afraid to seek help because they feel ashamed or fear repercussions from enraged spouses. However, the military has become increasingly responsive and sensitive to the issue of domestic violence, and there are capable and sensitive people ready to assist you, in addition to a vast array of resources in the civilian population, which are also available to you (see the sidebar in this section for details).

If you experience domestic violence, child abuse, or sexual assault, do not fall into the common trap of shame and guilt. It's not your fault. The first step is to physically remove yourself and your children to a safe place—perhaps a friend's or relative's home. Next, you can go through the military chain of command to report the abuse, a recommended course of action because it uses the resources most available to you. Studies have shown that when the abuser's commander gets involved, and talks to the case-review officers about the case, the outcome of reporting abuse tends to be a good one *both* for the abusive spouse *as well as* the victim or victims. If you fear financial penalties to the abusive spouse, which will also affect the rest of the family, the military has instituted a solution here as well, in the form of Transitional Compensation for the spouse and children (more information about this can be found at www.armycommunityservice.org/vacs_advocacy/data/modules/pbm/rendered/spouse_abuse_1.asp).

If you're still not ready to use these channels, you can take advantage of your six free visits to community counselors, paid for by the military (after that you would have to pay for any further sessions). Most visits are confidential, but keep in mind that a domestic violence disclosure may not be. Finally, if you fear disclosure, you can contact the confidential nationwide hotline that serves military as well as civilian survivors of abuse, and receive the benefits of advocates' crisis-counseling skills. You can also contact a military chaplain, who will keep your disclosure confidential. The point is to consider taking early action, because it tends to produce better outcomes for the family overall.

Survival Kit

For access to your self-referred six free visits to outside counselors, call 1-800-464-8107. To find a trained advocate through military channels who can help and support you, go to www.armycommunityservice.org/vacs_advocacy/home.asp. For *confidential* assistance and referrals in case of violence, call the national domestic violence hotline at 1-800-799-SAFE. You can also report domestic violence directly to the police, or at a hospital during treatment for injuries, or obtain a restraining order from a judge.

When the Reunion Ends

If the thought of your partner's next departure is a pleasant topic to both of you, don't feel guilty: the feeling is not uncommon among experienced military couples. "After seven months or so with our spouses, we start thinking: don't you have somewhere you need to be?" joked Joan. "Actually," she continued, "life is easier for us when our spouses are away. We love being with them, but our work doubles: there's twice the laundry, cooking to do every night after getting back from work, and more cleaning. So we're a little relieved when it's time for them to leave again."

For newer couples, and couples who see one partner returning to a war zone, the transition may be more fraught. Indeed, Veronica, an experienced military spouse, has never become inured to separation pangs. "I *hate* it when my husband's deployed," she said. Resilience to the situation comes with practice, but in the meantime, prepare for the deployment in all the ways described in this chapter. After your first such cycle of predeployment, deployment, and reunion, you will become more expert at navigating the transitions and on your way to becoming a resilient military spouse.

The Least You Need to Know

♦ When you get your deployment orders, make a financial plan and a communication plan, and prepare your family support system by introducing your partner to as many people as possible.

♦ Negotiate ground rules for commitment and fidelity with your partner.

♦ Keep track of your financial and other decisions; keep your children informed but positive.

♦ Avoid surprise reunions; prepare for reunions by slowly withdrawing from your "super-spouse" role and making room in decision-making for the returning spouse. The returning spouse, in turn, can prepare to relinquish the habit of command and obedience and get ready for a partnership.

♦ Your partner may return home changed; give him or her space and time to readjust.

♦ If your partner abuses you or your children, or seems dangerous, seek help immediately.

Chapter 10

A Partnership Over Time

In This Chapter

- ◆ Feeling secure about your LDR
- ◆ Tips for thinking about your LDR
- ◆ Taking care of each other across time and distance
- ◆ The special advantages of being in an LDR

It's certainly not your standard relationship, is it? As the months and years go by, the path ahead may not be clear, and LDR couples may become rattled by not knowing what the future holds. But before you gnaw off your fingernails, take heart in the fact that the future is not clear even to most same-location couples. The difference between LDRs and same-location couples is that the latter have the comfort of precedent: couples like them have been around a long time. So, they have self-acceptance and a certain confidence that they will make it through the uncertain future. My task in this chapter is to create the same kind of security, self-acceptance, and confidence for LDR couples, too.

In this chapter, I'll talk about how to be long-term partners in an LDR, including long-term challenges, advice on how to think about your LDR, caring for each other in illness, and finally some cool bonuses you have that other couples do not.

Security Blanket Needed!

Like Linus in the Charlie Brown comic strip, certain aspects of your LDR might make you long for a security blanket. Security is, after all, one of the most fundamental quests in human life, and the uncharted nature of LDR relationships might make you feel less than secure with the passage of time. Let's look at some of the things that make LDR couples look for that blanket, and take steps to provide one.

Increasing Entrenchment?

Well, suppose you took my advice from other parts of this book: created a comfortable living space for yourself, made friends in your locality, and kept two sets of everything—well, why stop there? You might buy your own house in mid-LDR, get a new car, and just build a life! And the more you build a life away from your partner, the harder it will be extricate yourself and have a joint life. Right? Right? To some extent, yes. The reluctance to become entrenched away from your partner is rooted in a healthy worry: you do not want to start "nesting" away from your partner. Dan put it this way: "You could build more and more of a life where you live, invest energy in people, accumulate more stuff, maybe even buy a home. So as time goes by it could get harder rather than easier for either person to move."

However, you cannot afford to let this worry drive you to the other extreme of putting *everything* on hold indefinitely, and not building any kind of life for yourself when you're apart. It's bad for your psychological health and it undermines your ability to be satisfied even with your relationship. The trick is to achieve equilibrium at a point between getting too settled and living in limbo. You don't have to get set in your ways, but neither do you want a barren life when you're apart. To this end, here are some tips:

♦ Make your surroundings comfortable, and keep two sets of furniture, kitchen things, and bedroom things. But don't go into debt for these things, and avoid accumulating the clutter you might acquire in a permanent home.

♦ Avoid buying a home for yourself in mid-LDR (except as an investment for the business-savvy). It's easy to get attached to a home and settle down away from your partner. If you buy a home *together* it is more doable, since you can both think of it as a main home, though it does tie down the partner living there to some extent. If you're not sure you'll settle in a particular town, rent.

♦ Use your "I don't want to get entrenched" sentiment to streamline your social energy rather than avoid expending it altogether. Use it to separate potential friends from people you'll keep at the acquaintance level. LDR partners can get good at making this assessment quickly. Make friends, good friends, wherever you can. You will not get overcommitted, nor lose these friends if and when you move. You're good at maintaining long-distance relationships, remember?

♦ Remember, you will stay intimate with your partner if you communicate well and maintain the quality of your relationship. Making yourself comfortable and having friends in another place cannot make you grow apart.

Don't let fears of becoming set in your ways prevent you from getting *slightly* to *moderately* entrenched. It's good for your well-being, and so, good for your LDR.

Postponing the Patter of Little Feet?

Here's a tough choice for bright, young, highly educated LDR couples: the most productive career-building years are also the most "fertile" years, and many LDR couples feel they cannot do both. Sometimes, couples know early on that they don't want kids, as happened with Dan and Erica, who were relieved to be in agreement on this issue while they were still dating. However, many dual-career LDRs fall into their career paths and postpone the baby discussion for later (after all, being together is just around the corner). There might be insecurity about dwindling prospects for having children as the years go by, but also a vague sense of a safety net because of the technologies available today. So many young couples feel like their baby options remain open even if they focus on their careers for now.

As the typical biological end of fertility approaches, and the prospect of having to use invasive technologies to get pregnant becomes more imminent, couples can start having that "Oh-my-gosh-we're-running-out-of-time" feeling. Kathy, for example, *thought* she didn't want a baby, but by the time she was in her late 30s and early 40s, and still working in Australia, she'd changed her mind. She wanted a baby, and she wanted a baby with Tim, who was in Indiana. She quickly took steps to breach the distance.

Here are a few pointers for LDR couples who are approaching the end of typically fertile years:

♦ Have the "baby talk" with your partner as soon as possible to get on the same page about how you feel about having kids.

♦ Make an appointment with your doctor to get your and your partner's plumbing checked out and get a professional opinion about your prospects.

♦ Discuss the results of your tests, and discuss your desires and options. For instance: do you want to have children (whether your own or adopted) while you're in an LDR? What's your timeline for any changes you want to make in your family?

> **Go the Distance**
>
> If you are postponing having kids during your LDR, as typically happens with young dual-income couples, one book you might want to read is *Taking Charge of Your Fertility* by Toni Weschler (see Appendix A). It gives you information and advice about your fertility, and is helpful to both men and women.

These tips will help you to take charge of the baby question instead of deferring it for later. Remember, too, that it is possible to raise kids in an LDR, as I've described in Chapter 8. It's a challenge, but LDR couples with kids rise to it. Some dual-career LDRs involve raising children, and military families routinely involve pregnancies, births, and kids growing up in LDRs. I'm not saying "listen, have a baby"; I'm saying "take charge of whether you plan on doing it, and when you'll do it."

Challenges That Remain Challenges

Studies show that (unfortunately for us) goodbyes do not get any easier over time. So manage your goodbyes as I've suggested in Chapter 3, instead of hoping that habit and repetition will blunt the emotional response to them. Get proactive.

Challenge number two is *feeling normal*. LDRs seldom feel normal simply with the passage of time. This is partly because of our own deep-seated expectations about relationships, and partly because family, friends, and co-workers typically respond to LDRs with worry, or as highly unusual. Having said that, there are things you can do to make yourself feel more comfortable: adopt some of the language in Chapters 15, 16, and 17 to talk about your LDR. Also, think of your LDR in ways I'll suggest in the next section, and convey some of these thoughts to people in your life. All these will reduce the feelings of being unmoored and different, and bring people in your life to greater acceptance of your LDR, both of which will help to alleviate the feelings of being beyond the norm.

Another thing that might not change on its own is getting fearful at night. This applies to the same-location partner more than the traveling partner, and it has to do with expectations. If you regard the place where you sleep as your "together" place, then suddenly being alone in that space after your partner leaves can spook you. You may find yourself double-checking doors and windows, keeping the phone handy, and performing other acts of caution that do not occur to you when your partner's there. To allay your fears, just remind yourself that it has to do with expectations rather than any real increases in risk. You're probably just as safe as always. It just feels different because you think deep down that your being alone in this space is unnatural.

Is There Enough Love?

As time goes by, there may be a niggling feeling in the back of your mind, never articulated, that perhaps there is not enough love in your wonderful relationship. For if there was enough love, wouldn't one of you have moved to be with the other? The doubts that other people convey to you might even accentuate any insecurity you feel on this matter.

Well, love does not equate to self-sacrifice. There are many facets of love, and maintaining a commitment *despite* distance is one of them.

You do not, after all, have an LDR because it's the easiest kind of relationship. You likely have an LDR because you love each other, and are heavily invested in prior commitments, which do not, at the moment, permit you to live together without near-complete self-sacrifice by one person for the other. This represents a practical problem, not a lack-of-love problem. It's true, as the song says, that love will find a way. But give it more time and keep your sense of humor about it.

> **Travel Advisory**
>
> People often cite distance as an after-the-fact explanation for why an LDR ended. However, LDRs that fail would likely have failed even in the same location, only sooner! Studies show that LDR couples are, on average, just as faithful, committed, close, and enduring as same-location couples. Remember this, and ignore the naysayers.

Solid or Weak Foundation?

Couples who have lived together for many years and begin an LDR later in life tend to feel more confident about the LDR. Why? Because they have greater reserves of together-memories to draw upon when they are apart. Those shared experiences are like a bank from which they draw interest that sustains the LDR. They are confident that their relationship has a solid foundation. Couples whose relationships *begin* as LDRs and continue as LDRs sometimes worry that they have a weak foundation, because they do not have all those years of shared life to look back on.

If you are in the latter category, take heart. There's absolutely no difference in the rate of survival between the former kind of LDR and the latter kind of LDR. Even if you and your partner have *never* lived together for long periods, your relationship is not at extra risk. Relationships that begin and continue as LDRs survive just as well as relationships that become LDRs after many years of living together. So, the feelings of confidence that older couples have when their relationship turns into an LDR can also be yours. There is every reason to believe that your relationship can stand the test of time just as well as any other. Besides, you, too, are building up a bank of together-memories every time you are with your partner. Imagine what a story you'll have to tell younger family members years from now, about all you have been through during your LDR. Yes, you *can* get to that point.

How to Think About Your LDR

Feeling unmoored and without a road map for your LDR as time goes by? There are certain specific ways to think of your LDR that are helpful over the long term. Let's touch on some of these ideas.

Temporary or Permanent?

Pam and her husband John think of the LDR as temporary. They talked about whether they could do an LDR when she first got the opportunity for her traveling job. They decided they could do it—for a while. Now, Pam has been doing the traveling job many years longer than she had initially thought. But she still thinks of the LDR as temporary. "I don't think I can do it for longer than two more years," she said. The prospect of the LDR ending is pleasant to her. There's no need to believe otherwise, and throw herself into pointless despair.

On the other hand, a woman I met on a plane described her LDR to me as permanent. She was traveling with two children. The three of them were having the most charming conversation, and I found myself wanting to talk to the mother. It turned out that she was like me, a professor, traveling back to work after visiting her husband. But she had children! "Do you think you'll ever live together?" I asked inquisitively (behaving just like nosy fellow passengers I complain about in Chapter 12). She shook her head: "No, he enjoys his work where he is, and for me, a tenure-track job is too precious to give up." I was silently astounded.

If you can think of your LDR as permanent without distress, as this lady seemed to, good for you. She is actually an exception. Studies show that most LDR partners cannot think of their LDR as permanent. It's too hard to imagine, much less accept, since it kills hope and thwarts the desire to live together, which most LDR couples harbor. LDR partners who try to talk themselves into accepting that their LDR is permanent stress out and go crazy, and eventually their heads explode (actually, they just stress out). Instead of asking for this unpleasantness, it's better to regard the LDR as temporary. The hope of being together keeps you positive, and staying positive helps your LDR. It's not just a trick, for it can motivate you to think outside the box (more on that in Chapter 19).

> ![CAUTION] **Travel Advisory** _____
>
> Avoid talking yourself into accepting a permanent LDR. You will likely not be able to wrap your mind around that concept, it is unwise to project your relationship that far ahead, and it may throw you into unnecessary despair. It's much easier and better for your mental health to break your future up into smaller chunks and take things six months, one year, or two years at a time.

A Sharper Distinction Between Work and Play

For many years, there's been a separation of work and play: people go to a separate office to work, and come home to family life. That dichotomy has in some ways only become more intense with time—people go away for work, work longer hours than ever, and come home for "quality" family time. Well, as LDR researchers have pointed out, an LDR is just a sharper expression of that dichotomy. The only difference with LDRs is that the work is far enough away that the work time and family time come in longer and more widely separated chunks. You are a commuting couple with a longer-than-usual commute. So think of your LDR as an example of a continuing trend of separating work and family life instead of thinking of your relationship as vastly different from others. From this perspective, it's really not.

The _Idea_ of Being Together

LDR researchers have also made a wonderful and fine point about the LDR experience. It is that being together is an inner state as well as an outer one. Most LDR partners feel coupled; carry their partner's voice, image, and memory around in their heads; and find their subjective experience of life shaped by the commitment to a partner. You know that someone cares about you deeply, and the affection is reciprocated. Even though that person is not always with you, the care and commitment make a difference to the shape of your daily life. So even though you may not be "doing" the relationship in the traditional way, you are still "being" in the relationship in a way that is subjectively meaningful, committed, and identity-shaping, just like same-location couples. Think of your LDR as "being" together even if you don't "do" life the way most couples do.

Taking Care of Each Other

LDR couples can take care of each other in all the situations that same-location couples do, in sickness and health, etc. For instance, when Marina had a tough week, Josh would hop on a bus and go see her that weekend. They had an LDR in which it was possible to travel without advance planning on any given weekend, so they were able to drop everything and see each other when one of them was ill or just wanted support.

Partner Sick or Injured?

You may not be able to spontaneously visit your partner in your own LDR, of course, and may have to develop other resources to care for each other during illness.

My partner once had a bike accident, got a ride home in a police car, and called me. I longed to do something for him but I was 3,000 miles away. He'd already received medical attention. So what I did instead, for the next few days, was attend to his meals long distance. I would call local restaurants we both liked, and have the food delivered to him during meal times. "That's the sweetest thing you could have done for me from there," he said, touched. I also sometimes called our local friends, and had them rally around during such times.

If your partner needs medical attention and you're not there, see if you can help by calling to schedule doctor appointments. If you need to coax your partner into seeing a doctor, attend to that promptly (but do not nag; respect your partner's wishes). If he or she gets sick while visiting, of course, nurse your partner—that goes without saying and you're probably already good at doing it! Also, it's wise to have emergency money available in case you have to pay unexpected medical bills or make a sudden trip to see your partner.

Survival Kit _____

Next time you visit, ask your partner's local friends and family if they would be willing to serve as support for your partner when he or she is ill or needs help. Get their contact info and keep it handy. Next time your partner requires support, you can use the list to have friends and family rally around when you cannot. Ask your partner to do the same for you, if it doesn't spontaneously occur to him or her!

Dark Nights of the Soul

If your partner is having a psychological crisis, listen, accept, avoid offering too much analysis, and focus on things that can boost your his or her confidence and feelings of safety. Don't judge, but offer words of compassion and real understanding. Above all, unless you are both used to therapists, don't treat your partner's crisis as some kind of aberration that requires the attention of a professional. Not everyone is comfortable spilling their guts to a stranger, and it's not necessary to make professional help the first resort when one of you is going through an inner upheaval. If you feel out of your depth, hang in there anyway, in the ways I've already described. Your partner is going through something human, and you are the one entrusted with the experience. So be human in return. The crisis is an opportunity for your partner to grow.

If the inner upheaval involves thoughts of suicide, however, contact a suicide hotline (1-800-SUICIDE) for advice on how to proceed. Also, if your partner becomes increasingly and severely depressed, gently suggest talking to a counselor or therapist. You can always ask your doctor for a referral, and interview the counselor or therapist before deciding whether to go ahead. Always remember that the most helpful thing you can do during a psychological crisis is to believe in your partner and offer a shoulder to lean on while he or she navigates the upheaval.

Visiting Patterns

The best way to have an LDR over the long term is to keep things sustainable, rather than ratcheting up stress over time. I touch on this in more depth in Chapter 15 on friendships. The trick is to keep your reunions and separations reliable, predictable, and rhythmic, as much as possible. Visiting more frequently is *not* as helpful as some of these other things; in fact, more frequent visits can wear both of you out if the visits are erratic and there's a lot of travel involved. Reliability, pre-dictability, and rhythm can better help you hit your stride, sustain your LDR, and take care of yourselves and each other in the long term.

Some Cool Pluses

Your LDR is an adventure that gives you and your partner pluses that other couples do not enjoy. You're *good* at certain things, because of certain challenges you've surmounted. Same-location couples take years to learn some of the things that are a natural part of your relationship. Let's dwell on these cool pluses, so that we can give ourselves a pat on the back for being so swell.

A Real Connection

You and your partner have a communication bonanza. Your LDR has forced you to become quick studies for how to communicate well. Silence across the dinner table? Not you! You've become experts at talking to each other, exploring your feelings, sharing ideas, bringing all kinds of outside stimulation into your relationship, enjoying your laughter, and enjoying special time in each other's company. Yes, being able to keep your relationship fresh is a great bonus. The cool thing is, the communication skills remain even when you start living together.

 Survival Kit

Make it a point to remember, and convey, the pluses of being in an LDR: better communication, less trivial conflict, more commitment, an ever-fresh relationship, more support of each other's dreams and goals, and the pride of pulling it off.

"Lean on Me"

You and your partner are good at supporting each other. After all, your LDR presents you with challenges that other couples do not face. Certain challenges you face alone, and your partner takes pride in them when he or she learns of them later and sees what you made of yourself.

Certain challenges you face together, and you learn to support each other as you navigate new territory together. Either way, you are experts at being a team, and this habit will stand you in good stead throughout your relationship.

Looking Back

Same-location couples often put one person's needs and career first, with the other partner sacrificing or compromising talent, opportunities, and personal growth for the greater good. Such commitment to the family is admirable, and to be respected. However, the sacrifices involve writing off deeper commitments today than they did in previous eras—commitments to one's own education (and debts undertaken to pay for it), talent, and productivity. They may also subject the partner making the sacrifices to isolation and despair. There can be regret in later years about the opportunities that one or both partners missed out on for the sake of the other.

In LDRs, especially dual-career LDRs, this regret is absent. Both partners experience opportunities. If somewhere down the line there is a compromise, there are fewer regrets, for neither partner feels deprived. The compromise is freely made after alternatives have been explored. So being in an LDR now can involve fewer regrets later on in life.

Most LDR couples, including the ones in this book, say that the LDR experience made them stronger and happier when they finally got together than might have been possible otherwise. Marina said, "I wouldn't *wish* a long-distance relationship on someone. But we're as happy as we are today because we were in a long-distance relationship. We learned about and supported each other through it." Ron said, "In retrospect, I wouldn't say I'm *glad* to have had the long-distance relationship, but I'd say if that was the path we had to take to be together, I'm glad we took it. Maybe, if we hadn't had that experience, we would have driven each other crazy!"

The Pride of Pulling It Off

You're in an LDR, something that few people attempt, and you're making it work! Take pride in it, advertise it, shout it from the rooftops, and give yourself a pat on the back, because you are indeed worthy.

The Least You Need to Know

- ◆ It's okay to get mildly to moderately entrenched in your life apart from your partner.

- ◆ Think of your LDR as temporary, and project into the future six months, one year, or two years at a time.

- ◆ Develop a local support system in both places so if your partner falls ill or needs support, you can contact friends and relatives in your partner's locality and rally them around.

- ◆ Your LDR makes you better communicators and a better team; you are pulling off something quite challenging, so take pride in it.

Taking Care of Yourself

Thought this book was going to be just about keeping the romance alive? Not a chance. This section is about taking care of you, *within* the LDR. The LDR, as everyone who's ever been in an LDR knows, can throw the rest of your life out of whack. That's why it's important to recognize warning signs and take care of you. To keep you sane and well, we'll touch on money matters, traveling well, and meeting your needs at different levels: physical, emotional, mental, and spiritual.

Chapter 11

Money Matters

In This Chapter

- ◆ Financial planning for your LDR's future
- ◆ How to take a year off to be with your partner and other financial strategies
- ◆ Tax breaks for being so swell
- ◆ When to drop bucks

Smart people can be financially dumb. Have you ever noticed that? I think I belonged in the "dumb" category when I met my partner, Dave. He brought me to my senses by expressing suitable shock at my credit card debts and conveying some elementary financial habits that he'd grown up with. Over the years, I have gotten better with money, which has helped our relationship in many practical ways.

Money is an area where LDR couples can think ahead, plan to take charge of finances, and benefit from doing so. Here, I will be discussing not high finance but just some ABCs of monthly paycheck management, so that your LDR is not being run by money concerns. The examples in the chapter are drawn from my LDR with Dave, because it seemed rude (not to mention dull) to ask the other couples who contributed to this book for their personal financial details. Finally, some parts of this chapter will be applicable to dual-income LDRs only, and others to all LDRs.

Money Is Important, So Plan for It

First of all, let's get rid of the notion that money is beneath notice. It's true that many of us choose our calling for reasons other than money. If I told you I was a philosophy teacher for the big bucks it brought into my life, you would laugh in my face. But it's a mistake to think that money is not a factor in your LDR. Money represents the resources you have at your command. Taking charge of it allows you to go beyond living paycheck to paycheck, and opens up future options for your LDR. Here are some goals and options for money management that will help your LDR.

Think Long Term

You're planning to be with this partner for a long time, right? Presumably, for the rest of your life. It's beneficial for both of you to make a financial plan early on, regardless of whether you keep your finances separate or undertake joint responsibility for them. Making a financial plan need not involve a visit to a professional whose first advice will be for you to fork over some money for *his* services before you even talk. It need only involve surveying your current financial situation and developing a strategy that allows you to maintain your LDR at a level of net financial gain, and perhaps bridge the distance over the long haul. Thinking long term allows you to make better decisions here and now about how you will allocate your money.

> **Go the Distance**
>
> The ABCs of money management, including budget worksheets and tips for creating a long-term plan, can be found at www.personalmoneymgmt. com.

Separate or Joint Accounts?

Whether and why you keep joint or separate accounts will likely depend on what constitutes the easiest way to manage money when you live apart, whether you are still dating or whether you are married, and each of your spending habits. Here are some of the options.

- You could keep completely separate accounts, and each pay your own travel expenses, bills, and debts.

- You could have a joint account for your joint expenses (perhaps a fund for travel, vacations, jointly undertaken debts and bills, etc.) and each have separate accounts for your individual expenses, debts, and discretionary spending.

- You could have a joint account at your main home, and the traveling partner could have a separate account at the town where he or she works and lives the rest of the time.

- You could have just one joint account into which both paychecks go, and draw your funds as needed from that pooled account.

The last option, having one joint account, works best if you and your partner have the same approach to money. If one of you has spending habits that the other cannot agree with, then one of the other systems is more advisable. Separate accounts have been lauded for promoting self-sufficiency and a sense of independence. Finally, in an LDR, a separate account for the traveling partner can help better track tax-related LDR expenses (which I'll touch on later in the chapter). In my LDR, Dave and I had different arrangements at different times. We initially had completely separate accounts; then just one joint account; then a joint account in one location with a separate account for me in the town where I worked. Discuss your options with your partner and see, based on your habits and dispositions, which system will work best for you, since different financial setups may apply at different phases in your LDR.

> ### Go the Distance
>
> For a discussion of the pros and accounts of different financial arrangements for couples, check out the website http://beginnersinvest.about.com/cs/personalfinance1/a/061001a_2.htm.

Don't Lose Money on Your LDR

How do you determine whether you're gaining, breaking even, or losing money in your LDR? The question usually comes up for dual-income

LDR couples who maintain two homes and two sets of bills. Here's one way to evaluate the finances. See how much money you would have for savings or debt reduction if one of you quit your job and moved to join the other, and both of you lived on *one income*. (If each partner is responsible for his or her own debts or savings, you'll come up with two figures, and if you've undertaken joint responsibility for finances, you'll come up with one.) Now see how much money you have for savings or debt reduction in your current LDR situation (again, you'll have two figures or one depending on your financial arrangement). Compare the figures in the two scenarios.

If you have more savings or debt-reduction money in your current LDR situation than you would if you lived together on one income, then your LDR is a financial gain. If you have the same amount for savings or debt reduction in your LDR as you would if you lived together on one income, then you're just breaking even. If you have less money for savings or debt reduction in your LDR than you would if you lived together on one income, then you're losing money on your LDR.

You might wonder why I'm comparing dual-career LDRs to living together on one income. After all, there's always the option of one partner quitting his or her job, moving to the other's location, and finding a job there. That might be the best financial situation of all. For instance, if your partner now puts aside $800 a month for savings or debt reduction, and you now put aside $1,000 a month for the same purpose, all you'd have to do to maximize financial gain is quit your job, move in with your partner, and find a job at your partner's location that pays more than $1,000 a month (since two can live almost as cheaply as one, and your partner's income already covers those living expenses).

However, this is not the most relevant comparison for many LDR couples. Maximizing financial gain is not every LDR couple's motivation. The motivation can be to maximize the *overall* benefits, taking into account finances, prior investments of time in one's career, future possibilities for success or advancement, and each partner's desires and aspirations for his or her life. Such considerations are often the reasons LDRs exist, as I've already mentioned in Chapters 2 and 10. LDR partners may not want to take any old job, or be underemployed, at the other partner's location, to maximize income. That's why I've asked you to compare the finances of being in the LDR to the finances of simply living together on one income. (If your motive *is* to maximize financial gain, you'd want to do the dual-income LDR vs. dual-income same location comparison to see which situation is financially better.)

If you're just breaking even or losing money in your relationship, it's time to develop better spending and saving habits. That's what the rest of this chapter is about.

Forego a Visit, Pay Off Debt

As long as you have debt, whether you are handling your debts individually or as a couple, your financial resources are not really your own. All your extra money really belongs to your creditor. If you fail to fork it over, your creditor will make you pay even more by charging you interest. Make it your first financial priority to work toward getting out of this situation. Becoming debt-free is the first step toward opening up future options for your relationship.

Some people ignore debts *because* they appear overwhelming. This is a bad idea. Once you start steadily paying them down, they become less overwhelming much faster than you might expect. To begin paying down debts, calculate your unavoidable expenses—perhaps rent, utilities, groceries, etc.—and reduce or eliminate the avoidable expenses—perhaps a car that involves big payments when a bicycle or the bus would serve your needs just as well; or a large, expensive apartment when a smaller one would be just as nice besides being less expensive. Then, after you've budgeted your expenses, see what's left over for debt reduction, and commit to paying down your debts by that fixed amount every month, whether it's $200, $500, or $1,000. The amount doesn't matter as much as the steady chipping away.

> **Counting the Minutes**
>
> Taking control of your money more quickly opens up options for the future of your LDR. Make reducing debt a priority. You can build travel to see your partner into your budget, but be willing to take fewer trips in the interest of having more money available for debt reduction.

It's important to remember that the longevity of your LDR does not depend on how often you see each other. It depends on the quality of your communication, your support system, and maintaining a positive attitude. So it is worth thinking long term, and foregoing a trip or two, to use the extra hundreds to pay off debt. If you adopt debt reduction and savings as a policy, you'll still visit, but you'll also pay off your debts faster and move toward greater independence. And greater financial independence is better for the long-term prospects of your LDR.

Budget Savings *and* Travel

When you've gotten on top of your debts, you can start saving all the money you previously put aside for debts. You're already in the habit of taking out a chunk for debt repayment. Well now, just take out the same chunk, but put it in a savings or money market account instead. You also have the option of budgeting some of your extra money for more LDR-related visits.

Here's an example of budgeting for savings as well as travel. By the time I got my first job as a professor, in California, Dave and I owned a home in Colorado and had no credit card debts. We only had a mortgage (which included a home-equity loan to pay for our cars) and my student loan. Since paying off the mortgage was a fruitless exercise—we'd be toothless by the time we were triumphantly mortgage-free and ready to focus on our LDR again—and since interest rates for my student loan were negligible, we decided not to overpay on the monthly mortgage payment or my student loan payment. Instead, we concentrated on savings and LDR-related travel.

I decided that travel to see Dave was non-negotiable, and I wanted to travel twice a month. So I budgeted $600 per month for LDR-related travel out of my anticipated paycheck. The rest of my paycheck would be available for rent, groceries, utilities, spending money, and savings. I found a pleasant and reasonably priced apartment in California, and settled in. When my paychecks started coming, I put aside the $600 for travel. After paying all my other bills, I found I could save $1,000 a month. Dave, at his end, was paying mortgage and other household bills, and socking away $600 a month. Between us, we saved $1,600 every month, and, because we'd budgeted for increased LDR-related travel, we also saw each other more often.

If you're not in the habit of budgeting, take a look at some of the financial software programs on your computer, or consider buying software if you don't already have it. It's easy to learn how to budget using your computer once you push through the initial discomfort of learning something new. After you begin budgeting, you'll likely find that there's more left over for discretionary spending than you had thought possible, as well. You won't feel broke because of that "pocket money," and when you're overspending, the budget numbers helped rein it in.

> **Go the Distance**
>
> Financial software may already be installed on your computer. Two popular ones are Microsoft Money and Quicken. More information about these programs can be found at www.microsoft.com/money/default.mspx and www.quicken.com.

Buying Time

Once you've paid down your debts and are saving, here are some other financial strategies to consider.

Get One Month Ahead

Instead of budgeting for this month's expenses with this month's paycheck, get one month ahead. Use bonuses, tax returns, and any extra income to buy yourself that extra month. Get into a budgeting pattern in which money from this month's paychecks will go toward *next* month's expenses, because you had already attended to this month's expenses the *previous* month. This is helpful if unforeseen expenses arise within your LDR—for instance if one of you gets sick and incurs medical bills or, more pleasantly, suddenly has something to celebrate, warranting an extra trip. If you've got this month's usual expenses squared away, and next month's money lying around, you can dip into that money now and compensate next month, perhaps with one less trip.

Make Good Use of the Credit Card

If you fly for your LDR, consider getting a credit card that gives you miles for every dollar spent. Such credit cards have an annual fee, so it's only worth getting if you acquire more miles than you'd be able to buy with your annual fee. If you get a credit card, use it to pay for everything, and save the receipts. Keep track of your credit card expenses by entering the expenses into your financial software program. When the credit card bill comes, you will be ready for it because you've tracked the expenses and set aside the money to pay that bill. And then, of course, *pay off the bill every month*.

There are many advantages to using such a credit card: you can accumulate miles toward free visits if it's a mileage card; you buy yourself time because you pay for what you bought only when the credit card bill comes several weeks later; and, you build a good credit record in the meantime.

> **Counting the Minutes**
>
> Many bills these days can be charged directly to your credit card or checking account, or paid online. Any one of these options will save you the time of licking stamps and writing checks. If you charge your bills to a credit card, remember to *pay off the balance each month.*

Our system was to have the credit card in Dave's name and put me on as a second user, so that we each got a card. We used the cards to pay for all daily expenses and most bills. Every month, Dave would pay off the balance. Since the balance would be quite large, including as it did both of our bills and travel expenses, I would write him a check to cover my share of it. We used the free miles, accumulated through credit card use and actual traveling, for an annual vacation abroad, but one could also use it for domestic travel to see each other.

Buy Yourself a Year Off

This is a truly sweet reward. Having enough money to be able to live at least one year without a paycheck is a good goal for anyone. But it's particularly nice in LDRs when one of you might actually want to *do* that—i.e., take a year off, be with your partner and make long-term plans at leisure, or plan a wedding or a baby. If you have a job in which you can continue some professional development on your own, or even if you don't, but simply want to buy time with your partner, it's an option to consider.

In your own LDR, aim for two things as goals: to pay down your debts, and to build up enough savings to live on for a year, should that ever become necessary or desirable.

Travel Advisory _____

> It's good to take charge of your money in the ways described here and in books devoted to the subject. However, just as ignoring money altogether makes it run your life, taking charge of it can make you excessively preoccupied with it. If you find yourself talking about money a lot, it's a sign of such preoccupation. Maintain healthy financial habits without getting absorbed in them.

When the Taxman Cometh

If you're married, there may be tax benefits to being in an LDR. For example, if you and your partner have a main residence in one place and one of you works elsewhere, you might be eligible for certain tax breaks, especially if the traveler has a contract job for which he or she had to leave home for some fixed duration. If you haven't already consulted a reliable tax preparer, it's advisable to talk to one at the beginning of the tax year. He or she can tell you what expenses to track. The traveling partner's rent or hotel bills, furniture rental or purchase, utilities, groceries, and much of the driving mileage may be tax deductible. When tax time comes, your tax person can advise you on whether it's more profitable for you to file jointly or separately.

In preparation for tax time:

♦ Keep all your receipts, organizing them by category; your tax preparer will tell you which receipts are needed.

♦ Keep track of each and every expense on your computer—the benefit during tax time is that your financial software program can give you the totals in each category your tax preparer asks for.

♦ Keep a small notebook and pen in your car, and get in the habit of logging the miles for every trip; make columns for date, purpose of trip, starting mileage and ending mileage; your tax preparer will tell you if any trips qualify for tax deductions.

This does not always mean you'll get big bucks back from the government, mind you, but it can mean you pay less than you would have otherwise. If you're allowed deductions, take them.

Paying for Peace of Mind

Once you have achieved stability and discipline in your finances, where you budget your expenses, pay off debt, and accumulate savings, you'll enjoy greater freedom and flexibility with your money, and you'll have a better sense of what spending is wasteful and what spending might be wise.

So far, I've talked about how to reduce debt and save. But there are also certain things worth dropping bucks for. If you have two incomes, you might as well benefit from them. If you've doubled your work by maintaining two homes, you can use your increased available income to reduce some of that work. It will enhance your peace of mind, reduce stress and keep you sane. If you build the following things into your monthly budget, it will not be money wasted, since it will enhance your well-being and bring relief into your busy lives.

Survival Kit

Be willing to pay more for peace of mind. Once you get in the habit of budgeting your money, you will be able to set aside money for it. House-cleaning help, yard help, a decent living space, and healthy food are examples of things worth dropping bucks for.

Consider a house-cleaning service for monthly house-cleaning help. This might be especially helpful for the partner who maintains your main residence, or perhaps raises kids. Just knowing that house maintenance will not fall entirely on your shoulders, that dust bunnies will not slide away from you in your distraction, can be a load off and worth the extra bucks.

Also consider yard help. If you fear loading your lawn with toxic chemicals, fear no more. These days there are many environmentally friendly yard services, which you can get by consulting your Yellow Pages and calling around. Or closer to home, there might be a neighborhood kid looking for extra spending money mowing lawns or shoveling snow.

For the traveling partner, it's worth dropping a few extra bucks on decent housing or hotel room, and a comfortable bed. Studies show that LDR couples in which one partner lived in substandard housing (relative to the other partner) were less fulfilled than LDR couples who lived in comparable housing. So while you need not match the size and luxury of your main home, make sure the traveling partner's housing is clean and pleasant. It's worth a few extra bucks for improved physical and psychological well-being.

Finally, drop a few bucks for healthy eating. When you're stressed out, your immune system gets depressed and you can get sick easier and faster. So it's best to err on the side of caution, and avoid foods that could increase your exposure to pesticides, hormones, and antibiotics. Drop a few extra bucks for organically farmed meat, dairy, and vegetables. Not only are they more ethically and environmentally "clean," but they also are healthy for you.

The Least You Need to Know

- Make paying down debts a priority even if it means sometimes foregoing a trip to see your partner.

- Think long term, and make it a goal to save enough to live on for one full year without a paycheck.

- In a married LDR, you might get some tax breaks, so consult a reputable tax preparer come tax time; in the meantime, keep records of your mileage and expenses, and save your receipts.

- Be willing to drop a few bucks for peace of mind; certain items like healthy food, house-cleaning help, yard help, and decent living space are worth the money.

Chapter 12

Traveling Well

In This Chapter

- ◆ General tips for travel
- ◆ Making it easier for the frequent flyer
- ◆ How to make travel time more comfortable
- ◆ On the open road

LDR couples always have great travel stories. Pam, who commutes every week, once missed the last connecting flight home and had to stay overnight in a hotel. She'd packed her toilet bag and clothes in her checked-in luggage, so she was in a bind. She decided, Well, I just won't sleep deeply tonight. I'll prepare to sleep light. She didn't want to disturb her makeup and suit. Looking presentable the next morning would carry more weight with the airline when she asked to be put on the first flight out, flown by a different carrier. It worked. In my own LDR, a friend accompanied me while I drove three hours from Lafayette, Indiana, to Chicago Midway airport. She'd agreed to drive my beat-up car back to Lafayette. Well, the car broke down on her way back. She found herself alone at night in freezing winds on a highway, with cornfields on either side. Fortunately, someone stopped to help. She was able to call a tow truck and find a ride home in a police car. Such are the dramas undergone by partners and their friends in LDRs.

Travel in LDRs is an emotional matter, with every delay, missed connection, breakdown, or other type of wrench in the works feeling momentous. This happens precisely because travel is for the sake of a dearly missed loved one, not business, and time with your partner is precious. Travel is such a prominent part of LDRs that it's almost like a third person in the relationship—not saying much, but demanding lots of energy. In this chapter, I'll talk about ways that people in LDRs travel. Then I'll focus on two of the most common modes, plane and car, and ways to make your trip more enjoyable.

Travel in LDRs

By air, by car, by road, by sea, by train, by truck—these are some of the ways LDR partners travel to see each other. Here are examples, followed by general tips for travel in LDRs.

Modes of Travel

By bus: For Marina and Josh, who commuted between Boston and New York, travel was on the Chinatown-to-Chinatown bus. "It wasn't very organized," said Josh. "Buying a ticket for the six o'clock bus didn't mean you had a seat on that bus. Sometimes you could only get on the last bus. The drivers often didn't speak English so they couldn't help much." Once, Marina got pushed and shoved aside so much while trying to get on buses that filled up before she could get on, that Josh had to protect her and muscle her forward in the line. She was weeping by the time she finally got on the last bus, late at night, several hours after she'd bought her ticket. "Parting must be very sad," said a sympathetic young man sitting next to her, who had observed her and Josh. "It's not the parting," said Marina, weeping. "I'm crying because it was so stressful to get on the bus!"

For LDR partners commuting between eastern cities, there are options other than the Chinatown-to-Chinatown bus, if you're willing to pay a bit more for a more pleasant journey. The Greyhound and Peter Pan buses offer safe, relatively smooth journeys between eastern cities.

By train: The train is an option in, and between, several states. Jack regularly took the train from Boston to New York in one of his LDRs. "I enjoyed it," he said. "It was relaxing. I would take my laptop and get an immense amount of work done, without distractions." There were big windows in the dining car, and passengers could watch the sunset, chat, and pass the time. Even today, I know people who travel from Manhattan to Boston for work every Monday, return from Boston to Manhattan on Fridays, and get an immense amount of reading, relaxing, and work done while traveling comfortably.

> **Go the Distance**
>
> Information about Peter Pan bus lines can be found at www.peterpanbus.com, and about Greyhound buses at www.greyhound.com.

By sea: Certain LDRs involve partners sailing away for several months, then sailing home for a few months. I speak of merchant marines and navy officers. There are often tearful group goodbyes from family and friends when they leave, and joyous group welcomes when they return. In these LDRs, travel doesn't amount to a commute. Being on board a ship is a career and a lifestyle for several months. The traveling partners see their partners and families during months off, when they live on land.

By truck: There are land-locked LDRs, too, where one partner's very livelihood involves movement. Truckers are a case in point. They settle into life on the road, and make themselves at home in the truck, shifting to another way of living. They may put a small bed in the truck, install various modes of communication so as to be connected with family, friends, and fellow truckers, and hit the road for work.

By plane: Plane travel has become more complicated since the terrorist attacks of 9/11. There are more rules, more rule followers, more security, and more paranoia around the whole enterprise. And yet, flying is probably one of the more common modes of transport for people in LDRs. Because flying is so common in LDRs, there's a section devoted to it later in this chapter.

> **Go the Distance**
>
> Research suggests that the frequency of visits has little bearing on happiness within an LDR or its longevity. So, if you cannot afford frequent travel, don't sweat it. Concentrate on other modes of communication outlined in Chapter 5, and on the quality of your relationship.

By car: Driving is also increasingly common in LDRs, especially among dual-career couples and couples in graduate school. Sometimes, the commuting relationship takes the form of one partner driving off for a workweek and returning for the weekend. Or it could take the form of making less frequent long drives to see each other. I'll deal with driving in more detail in the last part of this chapter. Before that, though, let's cover some other general aspects of travel in LDRs.

Time Is Precious

Travel eats up time, both for the traveler and the person waiting at the other end. So in LDRs that involve frequent travel, time can feel precious. During my LDR I once signed up for a writing workshop, which took up a five-hour chunk of time every week: one hour to drive there, a three-hour workshop session, and one hour to drive back. One evening, one of the other workshop participants blathered on for 45 minutes about a charity event unrelated to writing, and I quietly freaked out afterward with the teacher. She finally understood that for me, class time was hard won. With 16 hours a week traveling (door to door), several hours preparing for and recovering from travel, and 40 hours a week at my job, creating time for the workshop meant staying up into the wee hours doing my work. I was less inclined than most to politely listen while someone hijacked our workshop time. "I'll do a better job keeping us on track in future," the teacher promised. The promise (which she kept) meant a lot to me, since I experienced my nontravel time as very precious.

If you find your time becoming precious because of LDR travel—and this applies to the traveling as well as nontraveling partner, who might spend time cleaning up, doing airport pickups and dropoffs, and setting aside time for the traveler—speak up to those who do not realize it. Most people will take it into account, and adjust accordingly.

Tips for Smart Travel

Here are some rules of thumb important for traveling sanity in LDRs:

◆ Keep two sets of everything whenever possible. I cannot over-emphasize how helpful this is. Keep two sets of toiletries, two wardrobes, two sets of underwear, two hair dryers/razors, etc.—one set in each location. (I'd recommend a third kit of basic toiletries just for traveling with, in case you get stranded in transit.) For Pam, one of her two locations is in a hotel, and she puts her second set of possessions in a duffel bag and stores it in the hotel locker until she returns, a practice you might adopt if the situation applies to you. As a result of keeping two sets you can ...

◆ Travel light. You have a small number of things to carry—a change of clothes, some basic toiletries, work files, and laptop. You will be less agitated about packing if you have fewer things to pack. You will also avoid standing in lines having to check in luggage. When I started traveling light, I'd still go into automatic overdrive before a flight, in anticipation of headless-chicken packing behavior. Then I'd realize I didn't need to pack much at all, and deflate with relief. As I got used to traveling light, travel became a lot easier.

◆ Dress comfortably but well. Avoid business clothes unless you are going straight to a meeting. But do make yourself look (and smell) well groomed and presentable. In case there is a hitch while traveling, the way you present yourself makes a great difference when dealing with people.

◆ Make yourself comfortable while traveling. Take a neck-pillow, earplugs, snacks, water, a personal CD player, or whatever else you need to make the journey pleasant.

◆ Allow unstructured downtime after travel if possible. Ask your partner not to schedule social engagements and activities for a few hours, and take the time to unwind however you need to.

◆ Make travel plans that you can stick to. The desire to miss flights or, more generally, postpone departure, in order to prolong your time with your partner is common in LDRs, but the benefits of last-minute changes to your plans are not usually worth the cost. Details on why are in Chapter 3.

Survival Kit

Adopt the philosophy "Look nice, be nice." Dress comfortably, but presentably, when traveling. Be nice when things go wrong. People are more likely to cooperate with you if you look civilized and are pleasant.

These six tips will help make travel much easier. An additional tip, one I explore in detail in Chapter 11, is to keep track of your mileage and your travel-related expenses (including meals). They might come in handy during tax time.

Stress-Free Flying

For people in flying LDRs, the physical elements of flying—drives to the airport, airport shuttles, waiting in long lines, taking off shoes at security, the sounds, smells, and colors of the airport, the feel of the airplane—are a major presence in life. You might not talk about it much because it makes for dull social conversation. Yet the amount of time spent preparing to fly and actually doing it can be wildly disproportionate to how little people in LDRs talk about the experience. Here, we'll talk about it, and I'll offer some of the wonderful tips LDR couples share about how to make it easier.

Booking Your Ticket

Let's take it systematically. Several points come to mind when it comes to booking tickets. First, decide who should book tickets. It need not always be the traveler. Pam, for instance, travels every week, but her husband John makes the arrangements. It works well for them. He is a former frequent traveler, and now retired. So he has both the expertise to plan travel, and the time. Pam is self-employed, so she "pays" John and records an administrative fee for his work, useful at tax time. You can similarly share travel and planning tasks in your LDR.

 Survival Kit

Keep your visits regular and predictable. This allows you to get into a sustainable work-travel-visit rhythm with your partner—helpful to your sanity, your social life, and your health.

Start browsing for airfares a month or so before travel, and book the ticket at least three weeks before travel. In Kathy's and Tim's LDR, she would e-mail him from Sydney, letting him know at least a month in advance when exactly her work would be bringing her to the United States. Tim would then have a month to find himself some decent tickets to fly out and meet her where she was working. Browsing for airfares can be a pleasant way to pass downtime, since it can be enjoyable to plan the next meeting. Booking online is also usually cheaper than booking with a phone call to the airline or through a travel agent.

If you're flying out of a busy airport, consider booking an earlier flight even if your preference is for a later flight. That way, if the airline's overbooked, you can volunteer to take the next flight and get a voucher for a free round-trip for being so swell. Now, to be honest, this practice has never worked out for me. I've volunteered whenever the airline has asked, but never been asked to forego my seat, and so never been offered a free ticket for my pains. Most of the time I simply wished I had booked flights that gave me more time with my partner, Dave, instead of booking on the off chance of a free ticket that never materialized. But if your best flight time is during a popular time out of a busy airport, you might be luckier. Earlier flights are also more likely to leave on time, which is important if you have a connection.

Pick your seats at the time of booking your ticket. Most airline websites now allow you to do this, and it is a blessing for all, but particularly tall people, who like aisle or exit row seats.

See if the low fare you found for the upcoming trip is also available for *subsequent* trips, and if so book several tickets at once. I've discussed how to budget such travel in Chapter 11.

Finally, get on the e-mail lists of major carriers out of your airport, and sign up to be notified of weekend specials and last-minute discount fares.

Good luck booking your tickets! And I hope you find new tricks that I haven't yet learned about.

Before You Board

Remember how excited you were when you took your first flight? Well, much has changed since then. For one, it's become cheaper to fly, so airports are more crowded and lines are longer. For another, it takes more time to move through various security filters since 9/11 before you can finally board the plane. As a result, travel can become stressful unless you get proactive about managing yourself.

Survival Kit _____

Be flexible while flying. Here, more than other modes of travel, you depend on things beyond your control: weather, the moods of airline personnel, technology working properly, and fellow travelers. You cannot control these factors, but you can control how you conduct yourself. Expect some glitches and do not freak out in response to them. Take them in your stride and stay calm. If you don't make it to your destination on schedule, neither your relationship nor your life is about to end.

Kathy, who flew frequently for her job as well as for her LDR, takes an easygoing view of travel. This was a conscious decision. "It's best not to take things too seriously when you travel," she says. "It's better to go with the flow and take things as they come. If there are mechanical delays, well, it's best to view it as a lucky break that you didn't get on a defective plane. If you get delayed because of weather, don't sweat it. If you miss a connection, roll with it and see if you can make the next flight out." The point is that a flexible attitude toward flying will make things go a lot easier for you. Getting mad when things go wrong will only anger airline personnel who might otherwise have helped, and frustrate you further.

As far as actual tips before you board, here are some things to remember:

◆ Arrive early so that you have ample time to find parking, and enough buffer time for sluggish shuttle buses between the parking lot and the airport.

◆ If you have a connecting flight, consider checking your bag, especially if it's heavy, so you don't have to lug it around while you make your connection (but carry on your toiletries and perhaps a change of clothes). If you have direct flights, get a portable and functional carry-on bag that you can carry and fit overhead on your own.

◆ If you're not planning to work on the plane, consider packing your laptop with your clothes (padding it well) and checking it with your bag; I've done this often, and it works just fine. If you have concerns about lost luggage, of course, you will feel better carrying such items on board. It's your choice. If you are carrying your laptop on board, consider buying a laptop bag on wheels so that it's more mobile around the airport.

- In large airports, the security areas of the different terminals are sometimes connected by corridors, so you can go through security at *any* terminal. If your airport is like this, go through security at the least crowded terminal with the shortest security line. I've done it many times, and not many people seem to know it's allowed. (If you're not sure which terminal has the fastest/shortest security line, ask an airline employee.)

- When going through security, anticipate the requests: take off metal belts, keys, shoes, and jacket; take out your laptop; that way you can walk through without being delayed for an individual search later.

- If you have accrued enough miles to become Special To The Airline, always look for, or ask about, a security line just for "special passengers" (fill in whatever frequent flyer exalted status applies to you—mine was "Premier"). If such a line doesn't exist, sometimes airline personnel will allow you to go through the first- or business-class security line, which is usually shorter.

Needless to say (but I will say it anyway), do ensure that you've eaten something before you travel. Preferably, let it be home-cooked food. Otherwise, if you must eat at an airport restaurant, avoid fast-food outlets and eat a sandwich, soup, or salad, perhaps with yogurt and fruit.

On Board! (and After)

Ah, here I can give you quick and peerless advice (mined, of course, from the experiences of LDR peers). You have your aisle or window seat, I hope, and are well fed and are traveling light. Now let me mention a few things worth carrying on board, and some other suggestions.

Do invest in, or request as a gift (perhaps a pooled one), a noise-cancellation headset. The value of this cannot be known until it is tried. I received one as a Christmas present

CAUTION **Travel Advisory**

Jet lag can lead to agitation, insomnia, poor concentration, and general fatigue. Don't worsen jet lag by blowing off expert advice. Over time it will exact a toll. Avoid alcohol and caffeine before and during a flight. Drink water instead.

from my parents-in-law, and became so delighted that I wore it for several days even on the ground—walking to work, at the office, and so on. I had not realized how much travel stress can be reduced by simply eliminating the humming, throbbing, buzzing engine sounds that flood your ears throughout the flight, not to mention the sounds of loud conversations and crying babies (even if you love babies). You can put on your favorite soothing music and relax into a warm cocoon, or just have silence while you read or sleep. The headset is a wonderful aid to concentration if you are working on board, too. Check out noise-cancellation headsets at www.bose.com. Other companies make noise-reduction headsets as well, available through www.amazon.com electronics department. The headsets can be connected to your laptop, airplane audio outlet (during movies), CD player, or iPod, so they provide versatile entertainment while cutting out airplane noise.

Other things you might want to take on board are a sweater, a neck pillow, snacks, bottled water, and reading and writing materials.

Kathy considers the flight to be her own time, so she writes in her journal, reads, listens to music, and does creative writing. I heartily recommend this approach, for then you can recharge your inner batteries while traveling, instead of draining them. It is also a good time to catch up on correspondence (the snail mail kind, the benefits of which I enumerate in Chapter 5). If you must work, let it be work that doesn't tax your brain. I've sometimes carried work on board, and I've been most effective at it when I've been grading student papers, rather than doing scholarly research. But over time I've learned to place even fewer demands on myself while flying.

If you have a long flight, get up and walk around midway. I have tried doing those chair exercises, but don't see myself keeping up the practice—they feel too silly. But Kathy does them, and recommends doing them. Do what's most comfortable to you. Just make sure you move around a bit during a long flight.

Should you be chatty with fellow passengers? Be polite, but there's absolutely no travel etiquette that says you must respond when people want to chat through the flight. I used to be chatty. When questioned about my travel, I'd say I was going to see my husband. This inevitably aroused curiosity and led to more questions, which was fine until one day a family man made a pass. I shook him off, but was taken aback. That was my first inkling that some people might assume, wrongly, that my being in an LDR meant I was less than committed to Dave, and the last time I talked openly with fellow passengers. When my headphones are off, I'm friendly, but cagey with personal info.

When you travel to see your partner, giving yourself time to chill out is probably the best way to calm down after travel. Watch out for venting travel stresses upon arrival. When you're traveling away from your partner, back to work, consider doing what Pam did: "I'd have a protein shake with breakfast the morning after I traveled. Then I'd work through the day quite efficiently."

The Road Runner

Let's turn now to travel by car. Commuting by car takes many forms in an LDR. It can mean driving to be with your partner for the summer. It can mean having two residences, and driving to see your partner occasionally. Or it can involve driving to a different town for work during the week, perhaps living in a hotel or rented apartment, and coming home for the weekend.

One friend of mine regularly drove 12 hours to see his partner. The drive, to his mind, was symbolic of what he was willing to do for the relationship. One insight from him, useful for LDR partners, is that after a long drive, the traveler wants to be acknowledged for being willing to make a long journey to see the other. So if your partner drives a long way to see you, make sure you're home, and not distracted with other things, when he or she arrives. Have a comfort meal ready if possible, or ask your partner what he or she would like on arrival.

Avoid fatty, heavy, greasy fast food while traveling. You get very little exercise driving, and the fat may end up staying. Stop at restaurants instead and have a light meal. Also, avoid excessive junk food, like chips. Concentrate on healthy snacks like peanuts, cheese, fruit, and yogurt (for when you stop the car and have both hands free).

Long trips are a great opportunity to see friends and relatives, who are so important in the support systems that LDR couples require. Consider *not* driving straight through and taking a leisurely journey instead, perhaps driving six to eight hours a day with small breaks every two hours, and seeing people you know along the way. It makes the journey less stressful, more pleasurable, and keeps the people you love actively in your life (as I reiterate in Chapter 16). If your route doesn't take you past friends and relatives, stay at affordable, comfortable hotels where you can get a good night's sleep.

Counting the Minutes

Keep a small notebook in your car and log all your travel miles. Make columns for the date, where you went, the mileage at the beginning of the trip and the mileage at the end. Get in the habit of doing this for every trip, whether or not you think it will eventually be tax-deductible. You can figure that out later, but for now, keep the records. Also keep all travel-related receipts.

Just as flying once in a while can be a pleasant experience, but flying all the time is something that must be *managed*, so it is with driving. A driving trip once or twice a year can be a meditative, pleasant experience, but driving frequently becomes something that must be coped with and managed to reduce its impact. And, the impact of frequent driving can be considerable. It can affect the health of your spine, for example.

To minimize the impact of frequent driving, first reduce the amount of driving in your life if possible. Remember, frequency of visits doesn't seem to affect LDRs as much as the quality of communication, which can be achieved through other means. You do not have to daze yourself with frequent driving at the expense of your health. Talk with your partner and come up with a solution that will allow you to make the most of your time together and perhaps reduce the total commute for both of you. Finally, it's advisable to adopt ergonomic driving practices, and make the drive as comfortable as possible for your spine, the most vulnerable part of a frequent driver's body. For more information about driving and health, check out www.worksafesask.ca/files/ont_ohcow/driving.pdf or www.drivingergonomics.com.

The Least You Need to Know

♦ The quality of your communication is more important for your LDR than traveling frequently, especially if frequent travel is taking a toll on your well-being.

♦ Try and allow unstructured downtime after travel to help you unwind.

♦ Consider flying a time to recharge rather than drain your "batteries." Bring along whatever you need to make the trip comfortable.

♦ If possible, minimize the driving in an LDR. Come up with a solution that will allow you to make the most of your time together and perhaps reduce the total number of driving hours involved.

Chapter  13

Well-Being and Sanity

In This Chapter

- The most important messages of all
- Why you should lower your standards
- Attending to your living space
- Ideas for staying emotionally centered
- Seeking comfort in relationships
- Animal companionship

When you're in an LDR, you can get busy juggling your various spheres of life, taking care not to drop any. You can get pretty externalized. When this happens, pause, decompress, and rejuvenate. No one is stopping you from taking care of yourself, so it's just a matter of you actually doing it.

Taking care of yourself reduces stress. Why reduce stress? Well, because life is more pleasant without it, of course. But what about those people who thrive on stress and pressure? They cannot stand relaxing and being still. To them I'll say, think of the big picture. Long-term stress depresses your immune system, making you get sick more frequently and heal more slowly.

Studies have shown that stress also makes you age faster. Finally, stress *possibly* affects fertility. Rather than wait for scientists to be unanimous on the subject, I say just take care of yourself so that stress is not a factor in the first place. In this chapter, I'll talk about various ways to do just that.

The Two Most Important Messages

The two most important messages I can give you in this chapter, and indeed, in this book, are *You can do it* and *Ignore the naysayers*.

My LDR began when I started my Ph.D. program. Eager to finish up quickly, I took on a large course load. Within three weeks, I was overwhelmed. I felt I'd bitten off too much: an extra workload in a new town with new people, initial substandard housing with an unpleasant roommate, and a fiancé far away. At a graduate students' meeting, I expressed my overwhelmed state and said I might drop some classes. My colleagues clucked in sympathy. They were mostly a dark, pessimistic lot, and accepted my gloom as only fitting.

The next day, a young graduate student who had attended the meeting knocked on my office door. We hardly knew each other. "I heard what you said yesterday, and I wanted to tell you, you can do it," he said. "You can manage that many classes. You can manage all your other adjustments. You can manage your long-distance relationship. Don't listen to people who tell you otherwise. They will take four years to finish what you will do in two." He himself had, against all expectation, finished his coursework in one year while caring for his sick mother. He was like an angel, dropping from the sky to impart this bracing, hopeful message (I hardly saw him again). It turned my attitude around, and I did indeed meet my challenges. I was lucky to get that message. You're lucky, too. You're getting that message from me, right now: *you can do it*.

That experience brought home another message: Don't listen to naysayers. If you keep giving voice to your hardships, you will find sympathy from many quarters, especially if you are doing things that others have not attempted to do. Sympathy feels nice, but it can also foster a negative attitude toward the challenges in your life. Remember, you chose the challenges that an LDR brings. That means at some level, you believe you have the resources to meet them. Continue to believe, and ignore the naysayers.

Lower Your Standards

Meeting challenges does not mean you must do it all. Here it is, officially set down as a Good Idea: lower your standards. When you're in an LDR, large chunks of your time disappear. For the traveling partner, time is spent making travel plans, traveling, and decompressing from travel. For the noncommuting partner, time is spent with extra responsibilities at home, perhaps work and kids, and making time for the LDR. When you have more to do, without more time to do it, something's got to give. So lower your standards. Don't expect to do all the things you did before *and* maintain an LDR.

Silence Your Inner Perfectionist

What do you give up, and what do you keep? To figure this out, you must first silence your inner perfectionist. Some people are Type-A personalities: super-organized, detail-oriented, and able to master challenges by breaking them down into small, manageable chunks. They schedule everything, including time with friends, and are filled with purpose. I have great respect for Type-A personalities, since they achieve a great deal, are very disciplined, and always do a job well. People in LDRs are often Type-A personalities, either because they already were, or because juggling their LDR brings out the organizational and detail-oriented aspects of themselves.

Sometimes the inner perfectionist can be a hindrance to the big picture, and that is when you tell it to shut up. Not everything desirable in life can be achieved with more organization. Yet, your inner perfectionist, once it's brought to the fore, can linger on long after it's needed, like a demanding guest who decides it will be fun to chat with you all night. If you find yourself vacuuming at 2 A.M. or spend several hours unable to choose between airfares minimally different in price and

> **⚠ CAUTION**
>
> **Travel Advisory**
>
> Don't become consumed with achieving some maddening, elusive thing. If your thoughts possess you and you are unable to stop the momentum, pause, breathe, and remind yourself that you're not about to die. Distract yourself with a walk or by listening to some music. Or if you haven't eaten, eat. The feeling will subside.

schedule, your inner perfectionist is overstaying its welcome. Keep it firmly in check. Otherwise, it will sit on your head and nag, making you feel guilty about inconsequential things.

Eliminate the Unnecessary ...

Once you've put your inner perfectionist in place, figure out what to eliminate. An analogy with Peter Jackson, director of the movie *The Lord of the Rings*, comes to mind. Mr. Jackson and his scriptwriters had to streamline three long, rich, complex books into 9 or 10 hours of film. They took a step back from the books and asked themselves: What is the spine, the central story line? It was, they realized, the story of the Ring and its journey to Mordor. Once the spine was identified, the rest was elementary. Everything relevant to the journey of the Ring was essential to the movie. Further additions were desirable if they enriched the story. The rest was put in the DVD as optional material, or discarded. Apply this formula to your own life. Decide what's essential to the story of your life, what's desirable for its enrichment, what's optional, and what (or who) simply wastes your energy.

 Survival Kit _____

It's late, you're exhausted, and the house is a mess. There are dishes to do, papers all over your desk, and yucky presents from your cat on the carpet. Do the minimum that will allow you peace of mind, and then sleep. Your functionality depends more on getting rest than on having a tidy living space right away. You can do your tasks better the next morning when you spring out of bed, energized from a good night's sleep.

Before I moved for my job, my partner, Dave, would fondly plant vegetables every year. After I left, he had more work at home. He had the care of our barnlike house and our three cats, plus cooking, bills, laundry, and other chores while riding the LDR roller coaster. He streamlined by giving up the vegetable garden: too much work, and not central to life. He closed off rooms that didn't get used. When he shopped for new clothes, he bought ones that didn't need ironing. He concentrated on essentials: communication with me, healthy meals, caring for the cats, and paying bills. He cleaned the house and did yard work when he could manage it without stress. Sometimes, he paid professionals for help with both. (See Chapter 11 for when to drop bucks.) Much of this elimination occurs over time, but it won't happen unless you give yourself permission to let some things go. And do give yourself that permission. It will make your life more meaningful and more livable. Ask yourself:

◆ What can I eliminate from my day without personal or professional loss?

◆ And, if you're feeling particularly stressed out: Will I die if this doesn't happen the way I want right now? (The answer will always be "No.")

... While Meeting Your Responsibilities

Letting things go does not imply failing in your responsibilities. It's important to keep your word, do your job well, and nurture your relationships. The trick is to not overextend yourself by giving your word all over the place. At your job, for instance, understand what your responsibilities are, perhaps after discussing them with a trusted mentor. Any extra work you take on need only be by choice, with your full awareness. Pam, a highly organized LDR partner who has built a reputation for professional excellence, conveyed three streamlining questions she asks herself at work:

1. Is it my responsibility?

2. Can I delegate it?

3. Will it make a difference a year from now?

On a related note, it's important for people in LDRs (just as it is for people in general) to avoid overscheduling themselves. Allow for unstructured downtime: web surfing during lunch breaks, chatting by the water cooler for a few moments, or whatever. You are not a robot, so quit expecting yourself to function like one. You will end up taking the breaks you need one way or the other. By allowing for them, you will get less frustrated with your imperfections, and use the rest of your time more efficiently.

Your Living Space

Let's turn to your living space as an aspect of well-being. Some people, especially men, act as if it's sissy to attend to their living space. At the start of an LDR, if they are the ones moving away from shared space, they will rent themselves a dingy apartment, buy a mattress and a small TV, put sheets on the mattress, plunk the TV on a cardboard box, and call it good. Everything else—books, clothes, telephone, computer— gets strewn on the floor. Then they sit on their mattress with chopsticks and greasy Chinese takeout, watching football and wondering why they're so lonely.

This failure to make your living space comfortable comes partly from reluctance to become settled away from your partner, with two sets of everything. That would represent a tacit surrender to a permanent LDR, which few couples want. As Ariana eloquently puts it, "To buy two blue-handled black bristled hairbrushes instead of one would be some sort of acknowledgment of a situation that I try to keep secret from myself." I've seen people in LDRs live in this transitory state for months and even years, getting increasingly depressed. Strike a compromise between creating a permanent home and living out of a suitcase.

Substandard Housing Away from Home?

Research has shown that among people in LDRs, one partner often lives in substandard housing, at least in relation to the other. If you're reading this in the bookstore because you just had to bust out of your bleak living space, you're not alone. But research also shows that when partners lived in comparable housing, they were much happier within their LDRs. Interesting, no? It's another good reason to make yourself comfortable.

Have Some Creature Comforts

A good bed is the only requirement for a home that I would say is non-negotiable. Almost everything other than sleep—eating, relaxing, socializing, working—you can do outside your living space. But sleep, well, you do it where you live. So drop a few bucks and get a good bed. It goes a long way toward keeping you functional and healthy. Don't compromise it.

Let's think beyond the bed. Most LDR couples live with a constant feeling of being unmoored and adrift. This feeling can be much reduced by tailoring your living space to your tastes. It can be your sanctuary, a place to nourish yourself and recharge your batteries. It can meet basic requirements for well-being (other than good sleep) like mental stimulation, nourishing food, relaxation, interaction and social contact, retreat and rejuvenation. In short, it can be a space that brings you pleasure and peace. You will be less depressed in such a space, and not being depressed is good for your LDR. Make sense? But to make your space livable, you will have to snap out of your this-will-change-any-minute-so-what's-the-point mode.

> **Survival Kit** _____
>
> A decent living space goes a long way toward satisfying your basic physiological needs of movement, nutrition, rest, and sleep. When you first move, spend some time attending to your living space to make it habitable and comfortable.

A one- or two-bedroom apartment can be furnished quite cheaply. But if you're loath to drop bucks on furniture that you'll only need for a little while, there are three other options:

- Rent a furnished apartment. Many apartment complexes offer both furnished and unfurnished options. If you're making rental arrangements from a distance, ask detailed questions about the quality of the apartment and furniture, and even for photographs via e-mail.

- Consider renting furniture. It can be installed before you move in. Quality varies, so examine the available choices (which can often be viewed online). It adds to your rent, but saves the cost of buying or moving your own furniture, and for married couples, it may be a tax write-off (see Chapter 11 for more on finances). Others install it and others take it away when you're done with it, making it wholly convenient and good for sanity. Two furniture rental websites are www.rentfurniture.com and www.cort1.com.

- If you know people in the area you're moving to, consider borrowing furniture. Many people have extra furniture that they keep in storage or in the basement, which they're planning to give away or sell someday, or which they simply don't mind lending out. I have friends who have filled their homes with borrowed furniture, and I've done it myself. I sent e-mails in advance of moving, listing what I needed, and humbly asked for help. Many people responded and lent me some lovely pieces of furniture, including an antique china cabinet with a matching buffet (which I used as a clothes chest) and a tea table. I had a full home by the end, with only my bed to answer for. If you borrow furniture, be prepared to rent a truck and arrange moving yourself, and take good care of what's entrusted to you.

For couples in an LDR, it's okay to have two of something, like bookcases, wardrobes, TVs, stereos, or whatever you need for sanity and convenience. You are, after all, in two places, even if you share a main home. Remind yourself it doesn't mean the arrangement is permanent. When you're through with your second set of possessions, you can have a big garage sale. So do attend to your creature comforts.

Have a well-stocked refrigerator; silverware, utensils, pots and pans; comfortable sitting and relaxing space for at least two; a radio and DVD/TV; Internet access; caller ID to screen sales calls (which often flood people who are newly moved to an area); a place for your music and books; a clean, fully functional bathroom, complete with Q-tips; and personal items and decorations (for example, throw rugs, framed photographs, posters, objects personal to you and your partner). The last item might strike some as dubious. But you'll be surprised how much warmth and comfort it brings to have items of personal importance and self-expression around.

Survival Kit

Arrange your space to suit your needs, not to impress mythical dinner guests. Like your desk in the living room? Put it there. TV in the bathroom? Go for it. People in LDRs entertain, but you're the one living in the space. Don't be a slob, but tailor it to your tastes. Friends, and all decent people, will find this natural. Don't worry about the rest.

Overextended Self, Noisy Neighbor?

Here I'm talking about neighbors, landlords, and others close to your living space. Pay your rent or mortgage on time and be a decent neighbor. At the same time, remember you're juggling several things. Enjoy your neighbors, even befriend them, but don't tolerate trouble or noise.

Good rest helps sanity and well-being, so you can't afford to play games with it. If you're in an apartment, use your landlord. Now is the time. If you have no landlord, talk to troublesome people at the first sign of trouble. Your boundaries must be known in order to be respected, so speak up. Do not fear that if you complain, you will be perceived as shrill. You may be in that space only part-time, but you're paying for it, which entitles you to full consideration.

During my LDR, I tended to downplay my needs when it came to dealing with neighbors. I failed to take into account that the LDR introduced new factors in my life for which I needed to make adjustments. As a result, I sometimes accepted the flimsiest of my neighbor's needs as trumping even my most basic ones. For instance, I accepted TV noises that kept me up at night, or laundry noises that boomed through my vents at 1 A.M. (and, when I requested cessation, was met with a "I don't have anything to wear to work tomorrow.") even after long travel days. I came to my senses and appealed to my landlord, who knew of my LDR and intervened.

Politely, but firmly, be a squeaky wheel. Maybe your usual instinct would be, as mine was, to "massage" troublesome neighbors with niceness, or, as others might put it, be a wimp. But when you're in an LDR, the direct route is better.

> **Go the Distance**
>
> If it's noisy at night, here are options: (1) earplugs: these white puffs of synthetic chemical are surprisingly effective. Or try (2) white noise: it produces a hum to replace the noise. The sound of a fan can suffice. Some radio stations play white noise at night. CDs are available at www.whitenoise.com.

Keeping House, Solo

LDRs require that you learn to fend for yourself in ways you might not have had to before. When you live with your partner, you might fall into habits of traditional labor division. But in an LDR, you learn new tasks: cooking, assembling furniture and appliances, lifting and carrying, making repairs around the house, and so on. If you weren't too sure you could learn these new things, well, now you know better. You can. Such learning fosters a sense of independence and self-confidence, good for your relationship and your life, so take charge of your living space, be proud of your new skills and knowledge, and regard the challenges of keeping house as being beneficial to you.

Gathering Your Scattered Self

Having attended to your physical needs (except food and health, which I'll address in Chapter 14) let's turn to your mind, emotions, and, dare I say it, your soul. These delicate parts of you can easily be bullied into silence if you're running around tremendously busy and keeping a tight rein on yourself. Ever feel your neck and shoulders getting stiff? The tension is mostly emotional, and a sign that you are neglecting those needs. If you get emotionally centered, and understand what makes you tick, you have a better chance of dissolving this muscle ache. Attending to your mind, emotions, and soul aren't luxuries in your LDR. They are the very things that keep you sane and joyful within it. If you follow a spiritual tradition, like attending a church, synagogue, or temple, perhaps you already nurture your inner life, but here are some LDR-related points to consider on the subject.

The Fatigue Factor

When small things go wrong, they'll upset you more when you're tired. You might find yourself weeping, or fighting with your partner, and be unable to stop. Tiredness, and the resulting emotional wobbliness, may be unavoidable in an LDR, but if you're aware that some of your upset is due to fatigue, you may be able to distance yourself from it more quickly and forgive it more easily in others. Diffuse the negative energy by putting on music or going for a jog. Have food (and perhaps wine). Chill out, and then evaluate whether the matter that seemed so important is still an issue. If it is, you will find that your brief rest has miraculously equipped you to deal with it more calmly.

> **⚠ CAUTION**
>
> **Travel Advisory**
>
> Be conscious of your words. You're not going to eliminate stress by being in denial about it. But if you keep complaining and repeating, "It's hard!" your experiences will bear out your thesis. Instead, avoid speaking these complaining words, and indeed, contradict anyone who thrusts them at you.

Your tiredness and emotional wobbliness can also be anticipated. If there are times you must rest or work, make your needs known to those around you. Then, the chances of something unexpectedly going wrong will be much reduced.

Get Moving!

Couples in an LDR can be seized by a weird tunnel vision. Life can get narrower and narrower, until all that remains in your horizon is a hypnotic work-travel-see partner-travel-work-routine. It can also be a sedentary life, made more so by sitting in airplanes and cars and offices for long periods. To snap out of the hypnosis—and because creatures with muscles need to move—I suggest simply getting out of the house a bit. Not only does it expand your horizons, it also familiarizes you with a new place, builds a greater sense of security, and provides needed exercise.

Walk out your front door and strike out in new directions each day. Or pick up a hiking book about your area (I've found the Foghorn Outdoors series helpful) and get out of town. A hike in the woods can pull you out of tunnel vision and put things in perspective. Even in urban centers like Philadelphia, Boston, and San Francisco, there are outdoor options not far off. During my LDR stint in California, I spent many wonderful Saturdays in the company of sequoias or marine mammals, alone, or with Dave when he visited.

If you cannot bring yourself to muck around outside (and why not?), there's the next best thing, the gym. You can achieve the same benefits there as outdoors. Gyms these days offer many options, and you can swim, lift weights, or take an aerobics class. Or stick a tape into your VCR and exercise in your own space, as Pam does in her hotel room while traveling. Aim for at least 20 to 30 minutes of moving around every day. It releases feel-good endorphins, removes toxins, helps you sleep better, keeps you in shape, diffuses stress and negative emotions, increases clarity, keeps you healthy, and strengthens your immune system. It works off the pressures you have built up running around for your LDR, so get in the habit of getting out and moving about.

Getting Centered with Yoga

Yoga is truly wonderful for centering the scattered person in an LDR. I recall staying up nights after a hectic day of travel, preparing for my workweek. By dawn, I'd feel ready to collapse and sleep all day. A gentle yoga exercise would miraculously revive me, and I'd go through the day without mishap. Don't follow my lead on unhealthy habits like staying up working all night. But I do recommend the yoga. A friend of mine in an LDR also conveyed to me a surprising benefit that yoga had for her: "Yoga helped me become more connected to my emotions, and this made me more articulate." What a cool bonus!

> **Go the Distance**
>
> Most health clubs offer yoga classes. To find a yoga class near you, go to www.everythingyoga.com/studios.asp and type in your zip code. To learn basic yoga postures online, go to www.yogajournal.com/newtoyoga/864_1.cfm#1. If you'd prefer a yoga book, I recommend *Yoga Mind & Body*, by Sivananda Yoga Vedanta Center (see Appendix A).

Put Limits on TV and Shopping

TV in moderation can be relaxing. It provides mindless downtime, which LDR partners sometimes need. By all means, make time for shows that bring you particular pleasure. But beware of keeping it on indefinitely. Those flickering images can keep you transfixed. TV is a real trap for people in LDRs, who sometimes find tired and lonely evenings stretching before them. Too much TV shortens your attention span, encourages snacking and over-eating, discourages exercise, over-stimulates your brain, and keeps you externalized rather than centered. Avoid harming yourself in this way. Watch some TV if you like, but put a cap on how long you do it each day.

Business travelers in hotel rooms are at particular risk of watching too much TV. Studies show that the majority turn it on as they enter the room and turn it off only when they leave. It's understandable. The TV fills the room with human voices, comforting to the lonely traveler. Still, avoid reflexive TV-watching. Instead, divide your relaxation time between TV, music, reading, and exercise.

If you find voluntary shopping inexplicable, skip this paragraph. The rest of us have a perfect excuse to go out and shop: we need clothes, we need food, and toys can relax us. Also, there are birthdays and Christmases that need our attention. The flip side is that shopping can temporarily comfort us when we're feeling empty. People in LDRs, with their partners far away, can experience frequent emptiness. In some strange, cunning, primitive way, a glut of stuff seems to temporarily fill the hole. As long as you're not financially strapped, there's no harm in taking this sort of comfort occasionally. You don't even need to spend money. Pam, for example, always locates the mall wherever her projects take her, and finds it relaxing to walk around for an hour or so, window-shopping and checking out the sales. But avoid falling into a mindless shopping habit. It can crowd out other possibilities for more lasting fulfillment like building relationships, reading books, having a conversation, and personal-growth opportunities. Let your shopping be shopping-as-fun rather than shopping-as-need.

A Good Book

Reading does all the things TV doesn't. It increases your attention span, focuses your energy, stimulates (rather than overstimulates) your brain, and enriches you. With so many excellent writers around today, there's plenty of pleasure to be had for those who get in the reading habit. For people in LDRs, who find it so easy to become scattered, reading is an easy way to get moments of focus and peace. If you don't read much, I suggest you try the reading-for-enjoyment thing. Start with 15 minutes a day before bed, and see how you like it. Best-selling paperbacks are generally easy reading, so give those a try. Or, check out the staff picks at your local bookstore. If you and your LDR partner start reading the same books, it also gives you something new and stimulating to discuss.

Music and Dancing

Finally, if you find yourself experiencing life as joyless, maybe it's time to dance. Irrational exuberance is wonderful and snaps you out of taking yourself too seriously.

I don't mean going to a dance club, though it's an option. What I'm talking about is drawing the blinds, selecting your favorite tunes, and rocking out. No one is watching, so you dance freely, even gracelessly. What fun this is! You can dance away many an earnest sentiment and restore your sense of humor. Give yourself permission to be silly, and let go. It's good for you.

Relationships with Others

There is another aspect to emotional health: relationships. It's common for people in LDRs, especially couples who separate after first living together, to feel that they are somehow different. It's not just in your head. Few people understand LDRs, and many treat them as aberrant. This certainly affects well-being and sanity, so here I'll talk about navigating feelings of alienation to reconnect with others. (I'll deal with friends and social life in detail in Chapter 15.)

Here are some general points about maintaining ties with other humans even as you maintain your LDR:

- You're not weird for being in an LDR. Several million couples can relate to you. There's nothing wrong with your choices—they are part of how modern life is changing.

- Friends, relatives, and colleagues might not be able to keep up with your life. Are you here next weekend, or away? Are you busy, do you want contact from others, or not? Do you need sympathy, company, or privacy? They deal with their bafflement by waiting for signals from you. As a result ...

- Your telephone might go silent. This doesn't mean there's something wrong with your social skills or that nobody cares. Don't try to talk yourself into accepting such false beliefs with grace and maturity. You could go a little stir-crazy inventing convoluted rationalizations. Instead ...

Survival Kit

It sounds corny, but whenever you feel down, do draw on inner resources that have worked for you in the past. Remind yourself of challenges you have overcome. Note the things you are doing well. Note the new things you are trying out, which take courage. Realize, with growing confidence, that you rock.

◆ Confide in a good friend, or your LDR partner. If he or she is smart, this friend will say sweet things to you until you feel better. Talk to someone who brings you back into the fold of humanity. Then ...

◆ Start bridging the imaginary gulf between you and others. If you're feeling shy, express yourself with people you like. Pull back if you feel overextended, and slow down. Then reach out again.

◆ When you wish for contact, make contact. Don't talk yourself out of it. The impulse to reach out is a good one, so connect with someone whenever it occurs to you. Tell your friend what made you think of him or her. Usually, the recipient will be glad.

◆ Some people prefer to schedule their social lives. To accommodate them, be willing to do a little scheduling yourself. Set up lunch, or dinner, or whatever, a week or two in advance. Avoid the sudden puzzlement of being ready to party after a marathon work-session, only to find that everyone's disappeared.

◆ Interact often with, and pitch your tent close to, a friendly face. During one year of my LDR, I shared an office with someone who also had an LDR. We had great fun because we understood one another. We would commiserate and swap stories. We eventually rented apartments in the same complex. Similarly, Dave bonded with a friend in an LDR while I was gone. She understood him in ways our couple friends didn't. It was a great support.

◆ Aim for a good social life even when you're apart from your partner. Sometimes it's nice to retreat into a solitary bubble, but don't stay there too long. Keep in touch with people you like, and pat yourself on the back every time you venture outside your comfort zone. You are cultivating the skill of navigating social waters without your LDR partner. As people become closer to you, this becomes easier and easier.

Go the Distance
If you want contact with people who share your experience, try these LDR chat groups: www.geocities.com/lysh19; http://groups.yahoo.com/group/WishYouWereHere; and for truckers' partners: http://lists.topica.com/lists/TTCwomen.

Animal Friends

Research (that magic thing) has shown that affection between a human and animal is beneficial to both. It reduces stress, brings joy, provides companionship, and takes you out of your head—good for people in LDRs who frequently get tunnel vision. If you travel a lot, I'm not saying transplant your animal all over the place. I'm saying consider adopting an animal with your partner *if* you can give him a good home and take good care of him. If you adopt a dog, make sure you have time for him; if you adopt a cat, be willing to provide a scratching post and train him to claw it (rather than amputate his toes). An animal will fill many of your needs and help you relax. But ensure that you nurture the animal in return, for he or she has emotions and needs of his or her own. When I was in my LDR, I didn't adopt an animal because I was the one traveling. But Dave and I had cat companions in our main home, and, while away, I made friends with the cats in my apartment complex. I met the owners, and we looked out for each other. One kitty came by each evening. I looked forward to his visits, and my tiredness would instantly disappear when he arrived.

The Least You Need to Know

- Remember that you can do it: you have the resources to meet the LDR-related challenges you have undertaken.

- Quit striving for perfection in every detail; instead eliminate unnecessary drains on your energy.

- Put some creature comforts in your living space.

- Stay emotionally centered with exercise, reading, and yoga, and allow yourself the occasional release of dancing; avoid too much TV and shopping.

- Reach out whenever you wish for human contact.

- Develop a relationship with a companion animal if possible.

Chapter 14

Food and Nutrition

In This Chapter

◆ Common dietary traps for LDR partners

◆ Eating habits that benefit your LDR lifestyle

◆ A menu for your dining pleasure

◆ Must-have items for your kitchen

"I often ate cereal or a PBJ for dinner," said Marina. "I didn't feel like cooking just for myself." And her partner Josh? "I think he ate out a lot," said Marina. Kathy, who is vegetarian and works in the hotel industry, often ate her meals in the hotel cafeteria. Sharing a meal feels wonderful and eating alone feels bleak. As a result, it's easy to neglect nutrition and food altogether when you're apart, or eat out. However, if you're leading a high-pressure life, your immune system is already taxed. So it's doubly important to eat healthy and stay strong.

I never had a problem with devoting loving attention to my meals. It is because of my Indian upbringing, where devoting anything less than one or two hours to meal preparation is highly unusual. If I cook something quickly, it feels wrong, and I find myself making a few more dishes until I have cooked for the requisite time. I don't propose to turn you into a clone of myself. Cooking for one or two hours is not everyone's cup of tea. But I'll talk about some of the easier ways to develop healthy food and cooking habits in your LDR.

Health, Happiness, and Your LDR

Your body probably rebels at your schizophrenic diet. For several days, you are relaxed, eat well, laugh a lot, and generally have a wonderful mix of chemicals and hormones flowing through your bloodstream, all of them saying, "Ah! All is well!" Then you violently wrench yourself out of these good habits, your stress hormones start coursing through your veins, your brain sends crazy signals to your pituitary and other glands, and you start eating poorly and sitting around feeling sorry for yourself. "Ah," says your body, "All is not well," and then it promptly falls sick or gains weight or faces some other unfortunate health condition.

The way around such biological schizophrenia is to first keep a positive mental attitude towards your LDR and maintain your well-being and sanity as described in Chapter 13, and second, develop consistently good eating habits. These two things help you to stay healthy and happy within your LDR.

Travel Advisory _____

Studies show that the quality of meals in an LDR, especially when partners are apart, is lower than average. LDR partners often rely on TV dinners and take-out food when they're apart, compromising their health. Avoid this situation. Keep your meals regular through your reunion and separation patterns, and get in the habit of cooking healthy meals for yourself. You're worth the trouble!

Avoid Bad Habits

Sometimes your behavior can change your attitude. To that end, here are some things to avoid when you're apart from your LDR partner, and perhaps prone to sinking into some of these habits:

♦ **Avoid fast food.** When you're alone, it might be easy to slip into the fast-food habit. "I ate a lot of burgers in the beginning," said my partner, Dave. "It didn't feel good. It was just easy and cheap." Fast food is usually not healthy food. It's loaded with all the wrong kinds of fats and sugars, and the production and processing methods are not reassuring from a health standpoint. Moreover, enthusiastic servers encourage you to buy large portions of food and drink, so you could end up with a gargantuan meal. If you grew up being told to finish the food on your plate because of starving masses elsewhere, you will end up overeating.

♦ **Avoid skipping meals.** This causes hunger pangs that can lead to bingeing and also low blood sugar. Research shows that eating four or five small—and the operative word is small—meals is better than a few large ones for stabilizing blood sugar and controlling appetite, and that eating breakfast is especially important for good health.

♦ **Avoid watching too much TV.** Notice I did not say "don't eat meals in front of the TV." If your partner's away, and you have your meal ready, there's probably no harm in watching your favorite show while you eat; there may be little incentive to sit at the table. It's the converse I'm taking about: if you're in the habit of sitting on the couch watching a lot of TV, this may be bad for your diet, since there's a tendency to snack excessively in front of the TV. (If you use your TV-watching moments to stretch and do exercise, of course, this worry would not apply.)

♦ **Avoid eating out all the time.** Eating out a few times a week is a wonderful way to socialize. However, I have seen LDR partners whose kitchens are dead, cold areas because they eat out for every meal, from coffee and muffins in the morning to dinner at night. Eating out makes you spend more money on food, money that could be put to better use; it is less healthy than home-cooked food; and the portion sizes in restaurants can encourage you to overeat.

♦ **Avoid fad diets.** They come and go and often produce sudden sharp changes in your body. In an LDR, following dietary do's and don'ts prescribed by miracle diets will only add to your stress level and send your body into various states of unpleasant surprise.

Avoid these habits, and go for the good ones described next.

Embrace Good Food Habits

Embracing good food habits does not entail a new quest for perfection. Banish the thought from your mind. Rather, it's a way to comfort and nurture your body. It also does not entail rigidly avoiding junk food. Once in a while it's nice to eat junk (habanero potato chips happen to be my weakness). Nudge yourself gently toward better health by cultivating the following good habits:

- ◆ **Build an arsenal of recipes.** Do you have favorite home-cooked meals that you eat with your partner? Next time you're together, get those recipes down in writing. Eating meals that remind you of your partner can make you feel good, emotionally as well as physically. Do the same with other family members: ask for your favorite recipes. Many LDR partners get discouraged from cooking simply because they lack that arsenal. Once you have it, you can build your own repertoire of meals.

- ◆ **Familiarize yourself with the 2005 Food Pyramid Guide.** It's probably imperfect. Nevertheless, it's a trusted guide, aimed at reducing obesity among Americans and leading to greater health. The latest recommendations, which can be found online, suggest smaller portions and emphasize greens, lentils, beans, whole grains, nuts, fresh fruit, fish, and olive oil. The pyramid can be personalized for your age and height, and includes guidelines for vegetarian diets—helpful for people making a transition away from meat.

> **Go the Distance**
>
> The government's 2005 food guide, which includes guidelines for vegetarians and vegans, can be found at www.mypyramid.gov. (A spoof on the website, created by critics, can be found at www.mypyramid.org.)

- ◆ **Buy quality ingredients.** Organic food is slightly more expensive, which will generally induce you to plan your meals better and avoid waste and overeating. It's also attractive because the animals are treated with humaneness and not loaded up with hormones and antibiotics, the produce is pesticide-free, the stores and markets are pleasurable to visit, and the food comes from small family farms that are able to personally monitor production. Locate organic sources by visiting www.eatwellguide.org and entering your zip code. Farmers markets are also wonderful sources for such ingredients, and you can locate the ones closest to you at www.localharvest.org.

♦ **Occasionally cook with, or for, other people.** As your repertoire grows, you'll enjoy putting food on the table for others to eat. Invite people over to cook with you, or just have them over for dinner. (Just be aware it's not always wise to experiment with new dishes on guests.)

LDR partners often become more independent and learn new skills in an LDR; cooking is one of those skills. It's quite gratifying to become self-sufficient in this regard.

Planning Meals and Grocery Shopping

During our early years of marriage, Dave and I would find greens dissolving into slimy puddles in our fridge, or cheese growing strangely mossy. Disgusting, I know. It wasn't because we were not cooking. It was because we'd bought too much food. At some point, we said, "This is ridiculous," and changed our habits. In your own LDR, plan to spend money on good healthy food, but make sure it's well spent. Here's how.

A Simple Plan for Your Busy Life

Before you make a grocery list, make a menu for the week. Here's an example of one I might make:

Sun.: Upma [Indian brunch], black-eyed peas with spinach curry

Mon.: Leftover upma, lunch out, leftover dinner

Tues.: Cereal, sandwich, shrimp with lentils and salad

Wed.: Cereal, leftovers, bread-wine-cheese-fruit-olives-fish

Thurs.: Eggs, lunch out, soup and bread

Fri.: Eggs, leftovers, dinner out

Sat.: Brunch out, one-pot stew and rice

Notice that this menu is not very taxing from a cooking standpoint. It involves cooking four proper meals over the entire week, and one soup.

The rest consists of leftovers, meals out, and sandwiches. It includes meals that are healthy but quick and easy to prepare so you can still eat well on nights when you really don't feel like cooking. Anyone can deal with this much attention to food.

Next, make your grocery list based on your menu. If you have a dual-home LDR, planning your menu helps your LDR schedule: you can stay healthy when you're away from your partner, but avoid a fridge full of food gone bad when you return; you can plan for healthy meals alone as well as healthy meals together.

Keep in mind that making a menu doesn't mean you'll stick rigidly to it. It only means you have a certain number of meals for which you have the ingredients. You'll make those meals in any order depending on your mood, or even find other uses for the same ingredients, altering your menu. The menu is just a baseline that helps you avoid overshopping, keeps you within budget, and saves you those moments of opening your fridge door and staring blankly into the interior, wondering what you will eat today and deciding you'll just order pizza.

Counting the Minutes

Save time by cooking enough for two meals. That way you can freeze one of the meals to enjoy later.

Things to Have in Your Kitchen

Here I'm talking about equipment. As I've mentioned, it's a good idea to have two sets of everything in your LDR, especially things required for daily living. Stock your kitchen with plates, bowls, and silverware; a knife set; a set of cooking pots; storage containers for your spices, staple foods, and leftovers; a nonstick pan; cooking and serving implements; a blender, coffeemaker, steamer, toaster, and microwave; and a crock pot or pressure cooker.

This last item might be unfamiliar to many people, but it's well worth discovering. Pressure cookers are great for fast one-pot meals, saving you time and making your life easier. They are widely available at kitchen and department stores.

And Now for Some Recipes

These were some of my quicker meals during my LDR:

Italian finger food meal: For this you need a fresh (or freshly thawed and oven-warmed) baguette, fresh mozzarella, sun-dried tomato, smoked salmon or trout, apple slices, Greek olives, basil leaves, and olive oil. Just drizzle the olive oil on the bread and combine it with the other finger foods however you like. Sometimes I'd put capers and fresh onion slices on the fish; sometimes I'd forego the fish altogether, for the rest of the meal was rich enough. Pour yourself a glass of wine, and the leisurely image will be complete. These ingredients in sandwich bread also make a good lunch.

Steamed fish with vegetables: For this you need any firm-fleshed fish, olive oil, a fish rub of your choice, broccoli florets or asparagus spears, rice, fresh mozzarella, baby spinach leaves, balsamic vinegar, salt and pepper, and lemon juice. Rub the fish with olive oil and the fish rub (adding any other spices you deem would enhance it) and steam it with the broccoli or asparagus. Tear the fresh mozzarella into bite-size pieces and toss with the baby spinach. Make a salad dressing of equal parts olive oil and balsamic vinegar, salt, and pepper. When the fish and vegetables are ready, sprinkle them with lemon juice, season to taste with salt and pepper, and serve with rice and salad.

Survival Kit _____

Your LDR is an opportunity for you and your partner to expand your skills. This builds self-esteem and is good for you and your relationship. So if you're not accustomed to fixing healthy and tasty meals for yourself, the LDR situation is your opportunity to begin. It's necessary for your health. But it's also desirable as a feather in your cap.

Adopting better food habits may initially require thought. However, as the days go by, they will feel more natural and easy. You'll soon reap the benefits as you grow healthier, happier, and more energetic.

The Least You Need to Know

◆ Avoid bad eating habits whether you're together or apart: fast food, irregular meals, eating out all the time, snacking in front of the TV, and fad diets.

◆ Develop good habits, especially for when you're apart: develop a recipe arsenal, use healthy ingredients, and occasionally cook for or with other people.

◆ Plan your weekly menu before you go grocery shopping, and then make your grocery list according to that menu; this allows you to avoid an overstocked fridge with food that goes bad while you're traveling or alone.

◆ Have a well-stocked kitchen with all the things you need for eating comfortably and cooking your food.

Part 4

Friends, Family, and the Wider World

You have a web of connections, so don't forget about them! Your friends move in a world divided up into singles and couples, while you have become a bit of a social hybrid. I'll discuss how to navigate your social lives through the change. Your family, meanwhile, wonders and worries about you, and struggles to explain your LDR to *their* friends. Family ties are important, so we'll see how you can maintain them while helping your family understand your LDR. Finally, the world at work: do you talk about your LDR or not? How do you avoid becoming a workaholic when you're apart from your partner? I'll discuss how to stave off your Demon Worker aspect, so that you have time to create a life when you're apart.

Chapter 15

Friendships and Social Life

In This Chapter

- What changes you can expect
- Dealing with friends' reactions and concerns
- Bonding as a "single"
- Sustaining friendships as a couple

Here's a familiar situation: You're having a conversation with someone you just met. You mention your partner casually in the course of conversation. But once you mention your partner the other person asks, "Where is he today? Didn't he come with you?" and then the conversation veers off, with you bracing yourself to answer familiar questions and comments: "Wow! I've never heard of anyone doing that!" "How often do you see each other?" "I don't know how you manage it." "What does she do?" And the insidious "Can't she find a job here?"

Socially, we accommodate and understand singles, dating couples, married couples, single moms, gay couples, even single dads. But it seems the world does not yet have a mental concept of LDRs. It's best to anticipate the bafflement and be proactive about it, so that you can maintain your friendships and continue having a social life. That's what we'll cover in this chapter. Let's look at how social life changes for LDR partners, touching on what changes and why, what you can expect from friends, what you can do to support your partner, what you can do for your own social life, and your friendships as a couple.

What Changes, and Why?

Your LDR has two rhythms: one when you're together, one when you're apart. So you make many shifts, which demand time, attention, and energy. The changed pattern can alter other aspects of your life, including friendships and social life in general.

A "Hybrid" When You're Apart

As part of an LDR couple, you're a hybrid. You straddle the worlds of singles and couples, being neither wholly one nor the other, but somehow belonging to both. Unlike mythical hybrids like mermaids and centaurs, who seem to move in groups of their kind, you're not naturally thrown in with fellow LDR partners unless you're very lucky. So you might find yourself at a loose end: paired up, but socially single; single, but unavailable; not quite suitable for nights out with other singles on the prowl, but also breaking the symmetry of "couples" gatherings. Thus, your social life when you're apart may bring you challenges. However, this territory can be navigated, as we'll see.

Exclusive Together

When you're together, you might not even *want* to socialize. Why do that, when you can have this honeymoonlike reunion with your partner? LDR partners can be very protective of time together, and exclude the rest of the world. Of course, with that choice, your social life as a couple goes on hold. Further, without social ties at each other's locations, each of you may fear that if you relocate to join the other, you'll have no life outside your relationship. This dread might prolong your LDR unnecessarily. So it's best to weave some social time into your together time. Later in the chapter we'll see how.

Friends vs. Acquaintances

One of the distinctions that becomes sharper for LDR partners is the distinction between friends and acquaintances. Good friends may ask questions, and you'll accommodate them. But LDR partners lose patience with inquisitive acquaintances. Dan says, "My friends were very accepting and supportive of our relationship. Acquaintances would ask more questions, and I didn't waste my time on them." Small acts of thoughtfulness from acquaintances make a great difference in LDRs. If a new acquaintance refrains from getting inquisitive, make a note of that person. He or she is being respectful of your decisions, and may be someone with whom you can develop a deeper friendship.

The Questions That Keep Coming

Your friends might have a reaction to your status as a single-couple hybrid. Reactions from friends and acquaintances are expressed privately, to one partner or the other, seldom to both together. This already tells you that the reactions involve concerns and doubts. Let's tackle some friends' reactions and find a way to deal with them. (In Chapter 16, I'll do the same for reactions from family members.)

"When Is He (She) Going to Move?"

When Josh took his job in New York, Marina's friends began expressing doubts. "You're in Boston, he's graduated, and he's taking a job in New York? Why? Why didn't he look for a job in Boston?" These doubts rattled Marina. She would recount her friends' questions to Josh, and Josh sensed that she was asking him those questions herself. The fact that Marina's friends were airing and transmitting their doubts to Marina was frustrating to him.

In fact, Josh was not ready to settle down right after college. He'd always wanted to live in New York, and the best, highest-paying job offer had come from there. He'd just graduated, and was young. He wasn't ready to forego opportunities he'd worked for. So he didn't look for Boston jobs despite Marina being there. Marina made it clear she wasn't going to move again. She'd already moved twice to be close to him. Their LDR followed. However, it was a committed relationship.

Doubts from Marina's friends only made Marina insecure and Josh frustrated.

When friends give voice to your own insecurities, you have a choice between indulging those insecurities in conversations with friends, bringing up those insecurities with your partner, or just keeping the faith and ignoring both external and internal naysayers. The last is the best course. But if you must discuss, it's better to bring up insecurities with your partner than indulge them with friends. In general, staying positive about your LDR is good for you and for your relationship.

> **Travel Advisory**
>
> Don't be rattled by the doubts that your friends may convey. Know that LDRs have just as much chance of survival as any other relationship, and that you and your partner will get together when the moment is right.

"Why Do You Put Up with This?"

Even good friends can sometimes suggest that something is wrong with having an LDR in the first place. This can happen either because they suspect that their own relationship would not be able to sustain an LDR—probably an unfounded fear—or because they believe that an LDR signifies lack of commitment in the relationship—also an unfounded belief. Or they might notice that you are sad and missing your partner, and believe that suggesting a change is the way to help.

How to deal with these situations? First, avoid provoking a fight or trying to convince your friends of the rightness of your choices. That is not your job, and debating your decisions makes it look like it is. Just say "Everyone makes choices and compromises, and we made the choices and compromises that were right for our relationship." Let your friends know, with your neutral response, that criticism of your LDR, whether overt or implied, is not cool. (If you feel that it is worth saying more, make sure they are willing to treat what you say with respect.)

Second, adopt a healthy mental attitude toward friends' doubts. Understand why they don't get it, and give them rope to figure it out. Your friends might not be able to put themselves in your shoes. Perhaps their own relationship involves at least one partner having a portable career, which makes it easy for them to stay together without either one giving up hopes and dreams. Or perhaps it involves one partner putting potential on hold for the sake of the other's career. The point is, you know, better than they, whether you and your partner are committed, and whether your relationship is good. Give them the previously mentioned response and the chance to figure things out, and stay friends.

"What Are You Going to Do?"

Many LDR partners hope that a combination of diligence, favorable circumstances, and luck will help them be together at some point in the future. The positive attitude keeps them going. As a plan, however, it doesn't sound like much, since it depends on things outside your control lining up just right. So it can be maddening when friends ask (and keep asking), "What are you going to do?" "What are you going to do?" "What are you going to do?" or, for variety, "Let's hear your plan." LDR partners feel like saying "I don't *know!* Please stop asking! It just makes me feel bad."

When people asked such questions, I sometimes felt (especially if I was having a bad day) that it was ghoulish curiosity about other people's troubles. But even if the question was clearly well meant, it was not okay with me to treat my LDR as fodder for speculation or dinner conversation. There is absolutely no obligation to answer questions about your life just because people ask them. If someone says, "Let's hear your plan," you can respond with, "Oh, we're keeping that under wraps."

When friends express doubts or demand to know plans, they usually mean well. Perhaps they believe you are getting a raw deal, and you shouldn't put up with matters as they stand. Perhaps they believe you need a plan, and they can help with it if only you will tell them. When friends come with these motives, they believe they are duty-bound to communicate with you even if it means incurring your wrath. However, remember you are in charge. Use the strategies I've mentioned to nudge your friends toward greater acceptance and trust.

> **Survival Kit**
>
> Let "couple" friends know you are interested in socializing even without your partner. This can be reassuring to them. They might have been wondering if they were making you uncomfortable by inviting you into their coupled world when you're "single."

The time and manner of your confidences are of your own choosing. Keep channels of communication open, keep your friends, and keep an open heart toward them because they mean well. But know you need not answer every question posed to you.

Being Active Singles

LDR partners can have decent social lives apart if they want, and also support each other's friendships. Knowing your partner and knowing how you affect your partner both play a part in this.

Bust Out of That Shell

LDR partners may feel the temptation to withdraw from social activity for various reasons: less time and more responsibility, loss of motivation in the other's absence, and feelings of not fitting in with singles or couples. If you or your partner feel this way, you could rouse from inertia to push through these feelings, or withdraw and be comforted by that daily telephone call. Why go out on Friday nights, or any night for that matter, when you have that daily phone date?

If you suspect this is happening to one or both of you, be proactive about it. You do not need to talk at length every night. Going out with friends is healthy.

Travel Advisory ——

Social withdrawal is a natural response to the tunnel vision an LDR routine might create. If you think you or your partner are withdrawing, remind yourselves: Social contact always makes you feel good afterward; so it's better to attend, and not skip, the social activity no matter how reluctant you may feel initially.

Sometimes, my partner, Dave, would receive an invitation to a party or just an informal visit, and find his social withdrawal so strong that he didn't feel like going despite having the time. But he'd go anyway, "… because I didn't quite know how to decline. I didn't have anything else to do, so I had no good reason to decline," he said. Afterward, he'd return home thinking, That was great! What was wrong with me, that I didn't want to go? He added thoughtfully: "I suppose I lost motivation to do the very things that would have helped me feel better." He was fortunate to have friends who periodically reached out to him even though he seldom initiated contact.

The best way to break through a loneliness barrier is probably to issue invitations, and encourage your partner to do the same. (If you lack the desire or time to host gatherings but want to reciprocate invitations, invite your friends to join you for breakfast or lunch out. These are less expensive eating-out meals, so you can pick up the tab.) The best cure for thinking that no one loves you is realizing that others are just as appreciative of being asked to do things as you would be. This was brought home to me some years ago when my office-mate, who was also in an LDR, came over to dinner with three other people I had invited over. He said, "*Now* I understand why you have a social life and I don't. You *invite* people."

Criticize Not

During visits, if your partner introduces you to someone new, and you have mixed feelings about this person, avoid criticizing the person to your partner. Don't underestimate how much you can influence each other's perceptions. Criticize someone, and suddenly your partner sees that person through your eyes, and boom! The friendship is doomed from the start. Criticizing your partner's friends, and indeed your own friends, is probably a bad idea all around. But in an LDR, when your partner really requires a friendship network for social contact and support, it's particularly destabilizing.

Be supportive and friendly toward your partner's friends, whether they are singles, couples, or people of the opposite sex. Recognize that your partner requires social contact while you're gone, and his friends provide it.

Friends or You?

During Josh and Marina's LDR, all his time would be spoken for. He'd work all week, spend 10 hours on the bus, have a weekend with Marina, spend 10 hours on the bus, then work again. Or Marina would visit, which would keep his weekend equally full. "Sometimes," he said, "I'd miss my friends. I'd want to go for a Yankees game with them on a Saturday." But it would be a hard thing to break to Marina. "There would be disappointment." Josh said. "I always felt a bit guilty when I chose to spend time with my friends when both of us knew I could have gone to Boston to see her." Marina, although disappointed, never complained.

Sometimes, your partner might feel like skipping an LDR visit because he or she is missing local friends and wants to see them. This is not a sign that your partner prefers friends' company to yours. It's a sign that your partner feels an important dimension of life neglected, and wants to rectify the situation. When this happens, take it in your stride and plan social time for yourself, which is equally important.

Survival Kit

Studies show that the most intimate, satisfying, and enduring LDRs are ones in which partners have a supportive friends network.

Encourage Each Other's Social Lives

If one of you is more outgoing and the other more shy, accommodate that in your LDR. I tended to socialize when we were apart more often than Dave did but if I was out when he called, or had people over, he was never miffed. Sometimes I'd put him on the phone and he would chat with my friends. For my part, I could have done better with his social life. I never registered that Dave lost his social "oomph" in my absence, because he sounded happy whenever we talked. Had I been more aware, I could have encouraged his social life even from a distance.

In your own LDR, keep your partner's social life on your radar when you're apart, and encourage healthy social contact for each other. ("Of course," Dave qualified, "encouraging each other's social lives doesn't mean nagging about it.") Also, if you're going out, send a brief e-mail or leave your partner a message, so that his or her fantastic anticipation of a long phone call is not disappointed at the last minute.

Introduce Your Partner to Your Friends

Make time during visits to introduce your partner to your friends. It will reinforce your sense of a shared life, make a normally invisible aspect of your life vivid to your friends, and finally, alleviate worries about friends of the opposite sex. Be open about them and avoid white lies to "protect" your partner. "The devil you don't know is scary," said Dave. "I would imagine some sexy, intelligent, like-minded, and most of all, *present*, fellow in your life. Then I'd meet the person, and feel better about him."

Travel Advisory

Avoid freaking out if your partner has a close friend of the opposite sex. You are not always present, and your partner may need emotional and practical support of the kind that, if you lived together, you would normally provide. Within limits (of course) that role can be filled by a good friend. Support this friend's presence in your partner's life. The relationship dynamics will automatically change once you live together.

Relationships Based on Shared Interests

If you lack opportunities to meet new people, your best bet is to strengthen your bonds with already-existing friends and family. However, many LDR partners are able to form bonds with people when they're apart. Friendships are based on having interests and values in common, and these can extend beyond your stage-of-life interests and values.

Jack met people through his men's groups; Josh maintained his college friendships; Kathy had friends from the hotel industry; Christine had an active social life full of people from Youth Ministry and other work colleagues. I picked up threads with old friends who'd moved to my area, befriended fellow LDR partners and some couples who "adopted" me, and met people through various workshops I attended in my spare time. The point is, these bonds can develop based on common interests *other* than your stage of life and relationship. Focus on expanding your social horizons, and you'll find people filling it.

Socializing Together at Last!

When you're together, you might not *want* to socialize. You might want to float on a pleasant wave of honeymoonlike togetherness with your partner. However, having a social life when you visit each other is good. You develop your social chemistry together, and you help your partner's social life for the times when you're apart. Your visits are a good time to reciprocate those invitations, and maintain your social networks as a couple. Here are some things that help your social life together.

Mark This Down on Your Calendar

Plan your visit dates well in advance. That way, if someone asks your partner, "When's he (she) next going to be in town?" your partner will know what to say, and friends can invite you to join them on a particular date. If you cannot say when you're available, it makes you socially unreliable in a world where people schedule social activities. If you know each other's visiting dates well in advance, it's all to the good.

Stay Consistent

If your partner runs social plans by you on Monday, and you agree to them, you might feel quite differently about them on Friday after long travel. Your partner may understand and accommodate you. Still, the inconsistency can affect your social lives, since you will either break your word, or never commit firmly to anything. To avoid this, give your word advisedly, and then keep it. Occasional lapses are understandable, but be consistent as far as possible.

Plan to Entertain Together

When you plan travel in advance rather than at the last minute, you and your partner can also host gatherings and issue invitations in a timely manner. Pam and John plan so well that they are able to have parties during the holiday season, with lots of friends over. "When we have something going on for which we have to plan in advance, I sometimes make checklists and give them to John," she said. "While I'm away, he keeps quite busy following the checklist, and when I visit we prepare the house, cook and freeze food up to three weeks early. By the time the day arrives we're ready." You can anticipate even smaller gatherings this way, and it can be pleasant to plan them together.

Regular, Predictable Visits

As a rule of thumb it's good to keep your visits regular and predictable. That way, you can get into a rhythm of social life when you're apart as well as together. In this scenario, there can be occasional spur-of-the-moment visits, but they occur against a backdrop of regular or advance-notice visiting. Pam, for instance, returns home every Thursday night, and flies back to work every Sunday afternoon. When she's home, she works part of Friday. Her husband knows that she is available Friday evening and all of Saturday. Because they have established regular, predictable visits, they are able to have an active social life as a couple.

> **Survival Kit**
>
> If you have regular visits, identify a day when you'd be willing to socialize; for example, Saturday evening. This doesn't mean you must socialize every Saturday, just that if you do, both of you know Saturday is okay for it. The mutual understanding allows the same-location partner to make tentative plans with friends who want to see you.

Speak Up About Socializing

Out of consideration for you, your partner may refrain from adopting an active social policy without your explicit desire for it. So if you would like to be more social during visits, let your partner know. Further, you can specify how you'd like social plans to proceed. For instance, if you'd like your partner to run social plans by you before committing to them, make that known. If you don't require this, make that known as well. And ask your partner to clarify what he or she would like from you in that respect, too.

The Least You Need to Know

- Your social lives might change because you straddle the single-couple world when you're apart, and become protective of your time when you're together.

- Be prepared for questions and doubts about your LDR from your friends.

◆ Take social initiative, and form bonds based on common interests *other* than your stage of life and romantic status.

◆ Keep your visits regular and predictable as much as possible; being consistent and reliable helps your social lives together or apart, and helps you sustain a certain level of social activity.

Chapter 16

The Extended Family

In This Chapter

- Understanding your family's challenges
- Help for the puzzled family
- Maintaining strong family ties
- Dealing with unsupportive families

Studies show that LDR couples with strong family and friend networks have more intimate and happy LDRs than LDR couples without such ties. It's not really a surprise, is it? Still, sometimes it's necessary to state the obvious, since even obvious things may not occur to busy, preoccupied LDR partners. I covered raising children in LDR families in Chapter 8. Here, I'll describe other extended family experiences of LDR partners, and tell you how to make room for mutually supportive family ties in LDRs.

Challenges for Family

Imagine having a son or daughter who is in an LDR. Parents see your days and nights, weeks and months, in fact the entire lifestyle, becoming quite unfamiliar to what they themselves have experienced.

They might worry that your LDR is harming you, and worry even more because they see no end to the situation. Do you think they'll be affected? Sure.

Your families may be silent partners in your LDR, experiencing puzzlement, concern, emotional highs and lows, social challenges, and desire for more information about your lives. It's important to adopt practices to abate their concern and help them feel reassured that you and your partner are okay.

More Questions ...

Your parents and their friends may have lived through an era in which certain LDRs were common. If they lived through the Vietnam War, they can probably remember men getting drafted, sweethearts left behind, and sudden LDRs springing up in their social circle. However, few connect those kinds of LDRs, which were involuntary because of the draft, to contemporary dual-career LDRs, which can be baffling to family members precisely because they appear to be *chosen* rather than imposed. Why, they might wonder, would a couple stay apart when they could live together just by deciding to do so? Family members may have a challenging time understanding this.

Your parents' social circle is likely populated with other parents. Quite possibly, they are in the habit of asking after each other's kids, and what is going on in the kids' lives. It's innocuous and friendly. When your parents' friends ask after you, your parents have no reason to hide that you are in one place and your partner is another. It would be rude and odd to respond to friendly inquiries about how your children are doing with "That's none of your beeswax."

But once your LDR gets mentioned, your parents might have to brace themselves for a barrage of exclamations, comments, and questions from their friends—including the question of whether your marriage or partnership is in trouble. Or they may have to brace themselves for uncomfortable silence while everyone wonders how to respond to news of your LDR. Either way, they face assumptions that the LDR signifies something being wrong, and awkward social moments of their own.

Concern at High Alert

Your family members want the best for you. They might become concerned with your emotional ups and downs, the biological clocks ticking away, your crazy schedule, and you each having to fend for yourselves in ways you wouldn't if you were living together. They might only observe the costs, whereas you and your partner have a pretty good sense of the benefits—respect, new skills, opportunities, and fulfillment in certain areas—that you gain. However, seeing the costs, your family might feel anxious about you. Compounding this is the sense that neither you nor they might know how the LDR situation will end.

If you're an older couple in an LDR, with adult kids of your own, remember they, too, will face struggles to accommodate your LDR and perhaps wonder if all is well. Your adult kids might also miss having time with you. Pam, for instance, travels during the week, arrives home on Thursday night and works out of home on Friday. Her adult daughter, who lives in the same town, sometimes invites her out to lunch. Pam, steeped in paperwork, finds herself feeling guilty at the prospect of leaving work undone, and declining. So Pam's daughter has to do a bit more persuading to get Pam to spend time with her.

> **Go the Distance**
>
> For some interesting insights on maintaining healthy family relationships as adults, check out http://psychcentral.com/library/parents_kidsrel.htm.

Making It Work: Social Etiquette for Families

LDR couples can do a lot to educate their families about their relationship. Your parents have life experience and wisdom that can help you, but you know more about your relationship than they do. So there's much you can do to support them and, in turn, create family support for yourself, through communication.

Here are some things you can tell your family about LDRs:

◆ It's not that unusual. It is estimated that three million couples (that's six million people) are in long-distance relationships in the United States alone: single people, married people, seniors, dual-career couples, people who meet while traveling, people who meet online, people whose work involves travel, actors, politicians …

◆ Historically, there have always been long-distance relationships; they are just more common now because there are more couples where both people work, and the economy moves people around more easily than before.

◆ Studies on LDRs show that long-distance relationships survive and endure just as well as same-location relationships. The rates of endurance versus breakups in both kinds of relationships are just the same. Distance doesn't cause more people to break up.

The preceding points help put your LDR in a larger context and normalize it. Your family will feel better for knowing these things. These facts are also available to them if they feel like saying more to inquiring people.

It's useful for your family to be able to tell friends: "[He or she] commutes back and forth." This normalizes the relationship because commuting is a common enough phenomenon that people understand it. So even if one lives on the East coast and the other on the West coast, make it a point to tell family how often you visit, so they can truthfully say you commute.

A good, kindly friend might ask one of your family members "How do you feel about them working in different places?" (I suppose this applies to dual-career LDRs more than other kinds.) Here's a response one parent conveyed to me, when asked this question about her son and his wife: "I said, 'Well, if *my* daughter had invested a lot of time and energy preparing for a goal, and fulfilling it meant moving away, I wouldn't want to hold her back. That's how I think about my daughter-in-law's decisions, too.'" This response is compassionate towards both partners, so consider conveying similar language to your family.

> **Travel Advisory**
>
> Avoid blowing off communication about your LDR. Your family members are often questioned by *their* friends about it. Educate your family about LDRs in general and give some info about your LDR in particular—how often you talk, see each other, etc.—so that they can field questions from friends and others, and feel reassured about your commitment.

Remind family members that they need not answer questions about your LDR just because people ask them. They can put a cap on what is said. Here's a policy you can suggest. When family members are talking about you, they should keep information factual, narrating simply that your child is here, doing this, and the child's partner is there, doing that, and both are well. If anyone is inquisitive (or rude) enough to ask if something's wrong in the relationship, just ride a long silence to let them know the question is not cool, and then say, "No, I don't think so." (Family members may not be certain this is true, but adopting this policy is supportive to the child.)

"Yes, We Have a Plan"

In Chapter 15, I noted that you might constantly be asked by friends what you are going to do, as if you have a huge problem. It is, of course, unpleasant when people imply that you have a huge problem. At the same time, LDR couples might not feel they have a very good answer to the question. Your "plan" to live together can involve some combination of diligence, favorable circumstances, and luck. But since the hoped-for happy result involves some factors beyond your control, the "plan" might sound thin when spoken out loud, and be easy to deflate. Yet, keep in mind it makes a difference to family members to know that there *is* a plan, even without the details. It abates their high level of concern. At least (they might think) these two have a mutual understanding of how they will bridge the distance. At least they *want* to bridge the distance.

You might fear that once you let your family know that you have some strategy or plan in mind, that they will ask to know what it is, and then give unsolicited advice or convey doubt in more subtle ways ("Hmmmm. I see. This is a plan?"). But how much you share depends on how close you feel to the family member and the relationship you have with that person. You don't have to divulge anything you don't want to. But at minimum, do convey something along the lines of "We have a plan. It involves some things that aren't directly in our control, so we have to bide our time. But yes, we've discussed ideas and strategies for being together." It might feel like a stretch to call your possibly nebulous ideas "plans," but it is reassuring to your family to know that *something* has been discussed.

Make Your Commitment Obvious

Your family knows you spend many nights in different beds, eat meals in different locations, and even have two homes. So they might think, where's the relationship? Your family may have no idea of the extent that you relate, because you haven't bothered to let them know. Let them be aware of your commitment. Your family's concern about you can be greatly assuaged with information about how often you travel to see each other; how long and how often you talk; how often you *write*; the affection you harbor for each other (yes, express it freely before them); and what you do for each other.

Make Time for Your Adult Kids

Earlier I mentioned Pam's adult daughter, who invites her out to lunch when Pam's home, only to find Pam torn because she is steeped in paperwork. Pam's daughter then notes: "What you're saying is, you can't come out and play, aren't you mom?" Pam, stung by this reminder that work had been at risk of drowning out time with her daughter, puts it on hold and goes out to lunch. Her daughter's words make it easier for Pam to rearrange her schedule.

In your own LDR, if you have adult kids, anticipate your children's desire to see you when you're in town. Sometimes you will take a hit with piled-up work, but try to squeeze in family time anyway. Having it is important for your well-being and the well-being of those you love.

Nurturing Family Relations

It can be easy to postpone family time if you are busy in an LDR. Calls and visits can fall off. However, be aware that family time is good for both of you, as is keeping channels of communication active and open. Maintain relations with your in-laws, and be alert to relations between your partner and your own family. Here are some pointers.

Make Family Holidays Happen

Many LDR partners think of the LDR as temporary. With this attitude, they are able to defer or postpone many things (living together being, of course, the main and obvious one). However, do not defer family time with *either* of your families. During the usual family holidays, see family, and alternate if possible between your family and your partner's family. It is worth overextending yourself once or twice a year to do so. Here are some tips for LDR partners during family visits:

◆ Being a guest during family visits is usually easier than being a host, depending on the amount of travel involved and the amount of rest you can have at your destination. If you can rest at your destination, more travel during holidays can be worth it: you get important family time without getting completely frazzled. If you'll have to labor at your destination, consider offering to host, since you can stress out at your home just as easily as in someone else's home, without the bother of travel.

> **Survival Kit**
>
> When you plan a family visit, be sure to schedule exclusive time with your partner at each end of it. That way you can get used to being with your partner before family members flood your attention, and you can both wind down and let the visit "settle" after it's over.

◆ Hosting need not entail stressing out if you start preparing in advance. Start planning the family holiday, including menus and meals (which you can prepare in advance and freeze), several weeks in advance. When you are hosting, you and your partner do not have to plan and execute together. You can divide up tasks. Draw up a checklist two or three weeks in advance, decide who is doing what, and go to work. Getting ready for guests in small spurts is much more pleasant than doing it all in one long, stressful chunk.

◆ Be honest with family. They may be quite accommodating if you convey the challenges that family holidays represent. Let them know you need exclusive time with your partner before and after the family visit, that travel takes a toll, and that multiple transitions take time to adjust to. In practical terms, let them know if you require travel- or work-related help, or, if you are hosting, if you would like help with food and hosting responsibilities. If time is short, let them know that possibly, you won't be completely prepared for them (read: "the house will be a mess"). If they know these things, they can support you both practically and emotionally.

You and your partner will both be glad later on that you made time for family and squeezed in those holiday visits, even if one or both of you felt overextended at the time.

Present a United Front

When you communicate with family, yours or your partner's, present a united front about your lives as much as possible:

♦ Avoid saying things about your relationship that you wouldn't be comfortable saying in front of your partner.

♦ If there's something about your LDR on which you and your partner disagree, avoid making your case privately to family.

> **CAUTION**
>
> **Travel Advisory**
>
> Resist, and indeed contradict, family members who introduce doubt into your LDR. Although the family member may be motivated by worry, he or she is not helping. If someone feels impelled to offer advice or criticism, stay loyal to your partner, educate the family member, and politely end the discussion.

♦ Be supportive of your partner even if your family voices the exact insecurities that you yourself have about your LDR. You can raise those concerns with your partner later, but avoid entertaining them when they come up in conversations with others.

It is better for you and your family relationships if you have a united front with your partner. Families will know you are on the same page and can handle small problems that come up between you, and you will feel better about your LDR. Most importantly, you'll be developing good family habits with the practice.

"Call Your Family, Darling"

Jack says: "I was fortunate to have LDR partners who encouraged me to stay close with my family. I probably wouldn't have been as good about keeping in touch on my own." With his partners' support, Jack maintained contact even when his family disapproved of his partners, and didn't appear to take his LDRs seriously (for instance, they mixed up his partners' names with previous partners). Now that Jack is getting married for the first time, with his siblings mostly divorced, his parents are happily reconciled with Jack's decisions. "You know, I think you were right to wait," his mother said to him recently.

Dan, too, supported Erica's close family connections, both geographically and emotionally. "Erica's family lives nearby, and her best friends are in her family," said Dan. "It's like a busy, humming beehive of activity," he added with a smile. So after considering their future, Dan decided that he should be the one to move, and join Erica where she lived.

Christine supported Ron's family ties as well. Ron would drive 10 to 12 hours to see Christine. He could have driven straight through, which would have given Christine more time with him, but instead he broke off his journey to stay at his brother's place along the way. This was never a problem for Christine. Ron said: "My younger brother and I were able to bond as adults for the first time during those visits. He was old enough to understand me, and I was able to talk with him about my relationship. He even got to know Christine better because of it, through all the things I told him about her."

When Chie got pregnant, she was in the United States with Makoto. However, she had no family and friends to support her through her pregnancy, and so she expressed a desire to return to Japan through gestation and childbirth. Makoto had to stay in the United States for his job, and was torn about foregoing time with his new wife. But he supported Chie in her decision, even though it meant a second bout of long distance between them. He took the positive view that he would be less worried about her precisely because she would have her mother and a reliable home nurse nearby.

These are just some examples of how supportive partners behave. In your own LDR, encourage your partner to remain close with his or her family. Support time spent with family, even if it sometimes cuts into your together time; encourage phone calls to parents and siblings; encourage the healing of any rifts that exist.

Keep in Touch with In-Laws

This is not difficult: place an occasional call, send photographs, ask what's going on with them. They want to be involved in your lives, and this is good for both of you, so keep them in your lives. If your partner's too distracted in his LDR routine to give good news and updates about

Survival Kit

Keep family members up-to-date with your travel plans. Let them know when you are on the road, when you have flights, and itinerary details. If you are flying, they may even wish to track your flight, as my in-laws did when one of us traveled.

accomplishments and accolades, you be the bridge. Every family takes pride in the accomplishments of other family members; if your partner is too modest or too busy or both, why, then you can brag to your partner's family on his or her behalf about your partner's accomplishments instead. Family members appreciate it.

Your Partner's In-Law Relations

No matter how wonderful your partner's relations with your family, it's still a delicate relationship. Be aware that your partner may feel uncomfortable in certain situations. For instance, Josh and Marina grew up with each other's families and knew them well, but Josh would still feel different when his own mother gave him blunt opinions, than when Marina's mother did. "My mother would always let me know when she thought I was being a jerk," said Josh, "and so would her mother. It feels different when your own mother criticizes you, though, and when your girlfriend's mother does. I would get frustrated when her mother said certain things. On the whole, it helped keep me more honest, and my relations with Marina's mother are very good, but it made for some tension at the time."

Dan faced a different situation with Erica's family. When he moved to be with her, he quit his job and did not have one lined up in Erica's town. He planned to job hunt after he arrived. But he was also plunged into intense wedding plans on top of the moving, adjusting, and unpacking transitions. Suddenly, Erica's family was all around him. Possibly worried about his unemployment, and certainly speaking from concern, they would keep inquiring about his job search and hinting at opportunities they knew of, for which he could be applying. It wasn't easy on Dan to be questioned when he needed some slack.

Keep in mind it can be rough on your partner if your family takes their questions or judgments directly to your partner. When questions take your partner by surprise, he or she may not be able to articulate as well, and nervousness about in-laws can compound this handicap. Here are a few long-term solutions you might try to smooth relations between your partner and your family:

♦ If your family is putting pressure on your partner, avoid doing the same; give your partner space and support and feel free to tell your family, "Questions are okay, pressure is not."

♦ Avoid becoming an intermediary between your partner and your family—this can prevent a more long-term understanding between them, best achieved if they push through tensions and find a sustainable equilibrium. It's unwise, in general, to speak on behalf of one family member to another, unless asked.

♦ Anticipate your family's questions and concerns, and discuss with your partner the extent to which you can comfortably address them before they even come up.

♦ If you're close to your family, ask them to trust you and your partner and treat you as a team; you are adults, and your decisions are to be treated with respect.

Blessed with a Dysfunctional Family?

So far, I've been assuming your families are functional. What if yours is not? You can develop some strategies for your sanity. Here are some habits of dysfunctional families as they can affect your LDR. Recognizing them will help you deal with them:

♦ Criticizing your choice of partner and your LDR situation

♦ Indulging in unflattering personality analysis behind someone's back; if they are doing it to other family members, you know they might be doing it to you and your LDR

♦ Focusing on what's wrong, rather than emphasizing what's right about your LDR, your choices, and your life

♦ Feeling entitled to demand answers; unless you are still a dependent in the family, demands are out of bounds

♦ Meddling in your LDR

♦ Not bothering to show interest in your lives; e.g., ignoring calls, not responding to invitations, never initiating contact except to ask for something, not acknowledging your partner's presence in the larger family

♦ Lack of warmth, or selective warmth toward one partner and not the other

To be honest, not all of us avoid all these pitfalls all the time. However, for dysfunctional families, these things stem from *habit* rather than periodic personal lapses.

How to deal with a dysfunctional family? First, give your family a chance. Keep them in your lives without indulging in their bad habits: withdraw from personality discussions and quietly resist any meddling in your LDR. At the same time, keep your LDR visible. This persistence can sometimes break through barriers. Despite the fact that Jack's family was sometimes uncomfortable with his LDR partners for various reasons, and despite the fact that they never took his LDRs seriously enough to get his partners' names straight, Jack said, "I thought it was part of my role to educate my parents towards a different view. I came with my partner to family functions, and sometimes it made my family uncomfortable but I thought that was good for their growth." In the long term, Jack's persistence and continued connection with family paid off, for they are now supportive of his past and present decisions. I bring up Jack's family here not because it's dysfunctional, but because Jack's attitude helped create even better dynamics within it.

Travel Advisory

Do not encourage or take part in negative analysis of family members behind their backs. Would *you* enjoy knowing people were dissecting you or your relationships in your absence? By the same token, avoid doing it to others, even if the rest of your family is going at it full tilt.

However, if you sense that all your efforts are going into a vacuum, withdraw your emotional energy. You can continue to be supportive of your family, but from a greater distance than before. If your calls are going unanswered and the family's behavior is hard or hurtful, stop "asking for it." A good relationship with your partner can go a long way toward nourishing and fulfilling you, as can the relationships you develop with your partner's family and your friends. If your efforts with your own family weaken rather than strengthen you and your partner, focus on other, more nurturing, relationships in your life.

Remember that you are in charge. It is good to have supportive networks of family and friends—good for your LDR and good for you. But there is no duty to do things that bring you great and unnecessary pain. You are in charge, so you call the shots on how to expend your energy.

The Least You Need to Know

◆ Maintaining strong family ties is good for you and good for your LDR; support your family in turn by educating them about your relationship and giving them language to deal with questions they have.

◆ Avoid putting family time on hold; make time to regularly visit family members during holidays and other times.

◆ Encourage each other's closeness to family and develop good in-law relations.

◆ If your family continues to be unsupportive of your LDR despite your best efforts, you may need to withdraw your energy and put a little space between you.

Chapter 17

The World at Work

In This Chapter

- ◆ When and how to mention your LDR at work
- ◆ Flexible work options to discuss with your boss
- ◆ LDR concerns during a job interview
- ◆ The temptation to overwork and how to avoid it

If you build trust with your employer at work, you can create an environment that is supportive to your LDR. Although people in the United States and Canada work longer hours than people in most other countries, employers are increasingly recognizing that a happy employee is a more productive worker. So it's best to achieve a sustainable three-way marriage between yourself, your work, and your LDR.

In this chapter, I'll touch on various aspects of the work world as it relates to your LDR, from how your LDR features in an interview situation, through negotiating a supportive environment at work, to—can you believe this happens?—overwork.

On the Job

Is it a good idea to let it be known at work that you're in an LDR? After all, it might make your bosses worry that you won't stick around. Won't they wonder whether you'll jump ship to relocate and join your partner? The answer is, not necessarily. Let's examine work priorities, and see whether and how your LDR-related priorities can be integrated into them.

Focus on the Essentials

Your first priority at work is to focus on your capability to do the job, your commitment to doing it, and your intent to stick around to make a meaningful contribution. You may feel an internal pressure to disclose your LDR right away, either because you feel that failure to do so would be somehow deceptive, or because you're in a rush to secure concessions. Both are mistaken motives. First, about deception: The LDR is not a shameful thing that you must "confess" up front, as if it's going to negatively affect your job performance, because it's not (quite the contrary, as I'll touch on later). Second, about concessions: A rush to secure concessions to accommodate your LDR could backfire, because such requests can make you seem like a high-maintenance, demanding employee. Remember that your priority at work is to do your job well, and that rushing to tell about your LDR is neither necessary nor wise.

When, Why, and How to Mention Your LDR

Not everyone needs to make judgment calls about when to make disclosures about an LDR. "Everyone knew about Marina at work, probably right from the beginning," says Josh. "It was a very friendly environment so I didn't really have to think about it." However, others do have to make judgment calls. If you're not in an obviously friendly, informal, flexible environment, it's best to proceed more slowly.

It's important in any job to establish your trust and a good relationship with your boss. Your employers have to feel assured about your excellence at your job and know you for a team player who goes the extra mile. When it's clear that you make a contribution and your boss values and trusts you, it's a good time to broach the subject of your LDR. You may judge the moment right to ask whether the company has family-friendly policies. (Whether you are married or not, LDR accommodations will only come from a family-friendly company.)

Why mention the LDR at all? Well, primarily because an LDR-friendly workplace would make your life much easier and make you happier. But mentioning your LDR also helps your company. Studies show that the compartmentalization of work and play in LDRs is good for business. People in LDRs tend to work longer hours, and the geographic separation of work and personal life ensures that they are fully present at work when they are there. Studies have also shown that family-friendly policies in the workplace increase productivity and lower stress, absenteeism, and illness. So—assuming you're a good worker, of course—it is in your company's best interest to offer you options for accommodating your LDR. Your bosses may not have given LDRs a thought, nor considered that accommodating them is part of family friendliness and productivity; but the case can and should be made.

> **Go the Distance**
>
> Find research results about balancing work and family and tips for business and employees at the Canadian website www.labour.gov.sk.ca/family/INDEX.HTM.

When you are ready, mention that you are in an LDR, and give your boss several weeks to digest the information and get used to thinking of you as an LDR partner. After some time, have an informal discussion with your boss. Say something like, "My partner's in Podunk, and we're going to be commuting to see each other. There will be weeks and weekends when [he or she] travels to see me here, and times when I travel there. If I get my work done as always, would it be possible to receive some flexibility about my time during visits?" Your goal is to secure the same recognition for your LDR as any other work-family situation that is already accommodated in the business world, such as pregnancy, maternity leave, the care of aged or sick parents, and the care of small children by working parents.

Give-and-Take Arrangements

Some jobs are more organized and require more teamwork, and some are more autonomous and flexible. LDR-related accommodations depend on what kind of fixed hours your work *requires* of you. Be reasonable in your requests. Here are some arrangements you might discuss with your boss, depending on the nature of your job:

◆ **Working from a remote location.** This is an option if much of your work can be done on your own, or on the Internet. Josh was able to use this option on days when he got snowed in with Marina in Boston, and was unable to return to New York by Monday.

◆ **Virtual presence.** If you're a teacher required to have office hours, you can ask that one or more of them be "virtual"—that is, where you're available over e-mail for the entire hour, with students knowing that you're available, and able to use that window to contact you.

> **Counting the Minutes**
>
> When the moment is right, disclosing your LDR and coming to a flexible give-and-take arrangement with your boss saves you the time and effort of tedious explanations requesting flexibility before each visit.

◆ **Teleconferencing.** Can you attend meetings via a conference call? Hotel industry employees, professors, CEOs, and publishers—in short, all manner of people—have accommodated their LDRs in this way.

◆ **Occasionally skipping a routine meeting.** If a meeting is a routine debriefing, rather than for a specific project, and it occurs just when it's optimal for you to catch a flight, respectfully ask your boss whether you can submit your ideas in advance, read the meeting minutes on your return or via e-mail, and have informal discussions afterward on the topics covered. If you speak with your boss about this in advance, he or she may be willing to accommodate you.

◆ **Catching up later.** If you come in on weekends, or work late on remaining weekdays, can you leave early Friday and come to work late on Monday? If you've used up your vacation days and miss a day of work, can you make it up without being docked for taking an illegal vacation day? This comes in handy if you're snowed in during a visit or return flights are canceled.

♦ **Working out alternative hours.** Almost 30 percent of workers in the United States have worked out alternatives to the five-day, 9-to-5 workweek with their bosses. A person expected to put in 40 hours a week could work 10 hours a day Monday through Thursday and have a three-day weekend after. Or a person could come in for work on Saturdays, and take Sunday and Monday off, as Kathy did in her job. Would your supervisors consider such options for you?

♦ **Short notice.** When you've established yourself as reliable and your boss knows you're in an LDR, you can occasionally go to your boss with: "I found a great last-minute airfare. Do you mind if I book that ticket and leave early to catch the flight?" Assuming you do not abuse the privilege by making it a habit, your boss may be willing to accommodate you.

♦ **Respecting your time.** Once your boss starts accommodating your LDR, he or she might respect your time in various ways. For example, he or she might check with you before committing you to a weekend meeting, inquire whether this is an LDR weekend before setting deadlines for projects, and refrain from contacting you on LDR weekends unless it's an absolute emergency.

Don't forget the "give" part of "give and take." Tell your boss, "I really appreciate your accommodating me this way. I just want to assure you that I'm committed to doing the job excellently and putting in my hours of work to meet deadlines and get the work done. Thanks so much for your flexibility." Following the discussion, of course, your task is to be flexible and conscientious: do your job and do it well; catch up on those missed meetings as promised; and work late or come in early to make up for LDR-related lost time. It's a good faith arrangement, so repay your boss' goodwill with your own.

Travel Advisory

Once your boss and colleagues know about your LDR, there may be some gossip about it. Avoid engaging with insensitive colleagues who let you know that *they* would never tolerate a long-distance relationship. Just say "That was our choice" and move on. If you have to work with them closely, let them know that your personal decisions are off limits for your working relationship.

Gimme This Job (Please)

LDR partners may switch jobs in mid-LDR without changing the long-distance nature of the relationship. One LDR partner who contributed to this book was invited to interview for a job in Phoenix. When he talked to his wife about it, she said, "It'll be just as easy for me to commute to Phoenix as to LA, so go for it." He interviewed, and was invited back for a second interview with his partner. Over cocktails and dinner, their LDR status came up soon enough and their plans were questioned—would she move, what did she plan to do, etc. The couple dithered away, unwilling to say "We haven't decided yet" for fear that this would make the candidate appear unstable to the interviewers, but not knowing what confident answer to give instead because they hadn't discussed how to handle such questions. The job didn't come through, and the couple soon learned to plan for LDR-related questions. Here I'll touch on interview-related considerations for your LDR and how to handle those questions.

What the Interviewer Seeks

The interviewer wants to know three things: whether you're qualified for the job, whether you're committed to doing it well, and whether you'll stick around to do it for at least a few years. They're also interested in seeing whether you're a congenial person, whether you'll be willing to travel for the job if that's required, and whether you'll go the extra mile when it's necessary. They do not care whether you're in an LDR, as long as it doesn't interfere with your job performance.

Despite laws prohibiting sexism while hiring, it can creep in. Female interviewees, in particular, might arouse suspicion by dwelling on their LDRs. The interviewer might wonder if you'll eventually throw in the towel to join your partner, especially if you appear to be concerned about your personal life. For women, like all other candidates, the LDR need not enter the interview, and should be dispatched briefly if it does.

Answer the Real Question Behind the Question

If the interviewer asks about your LDR, he or she may be trying to determine whether you plan to stick around, and whether you'll go the extra mile for the job. When such questions come up, recognize what the interviewer is really getting at, and avoid overexplaining. The objective is to offer brief, truthful answers that cut off the topic and allow you to reassure the employer on job-related considerations. Here are a few tips:

◆ If asked about your personal plans, focus on *actions*, not *outcomes*. For example, if asked whether your partner will join you, say "She will keep her current job but will look for jobs here," *not* "We plan to end up living here together" (with the latter you might as well be adding, "we're not sure how we'll swing it; ask me more questions, and also, feel free to get alarmed and consider me an unstable prospect"). Say "There will be a transition period between me and my partner when I move here, but that will not affect my start date," *not* "We'll have to figure out the logistics of our relationship with my move for this job, so I might need more time before my start date" (with the latter, you might as well be saying, "Is it okay if my personal life inconveniences you?").

◆ If someone asks about your partner, keep your answer factual rather than speculative. The interviewer does not have a right to know about your LDR. The interviewer *does* have the right to determine your ability and motivation to do the job, and this may be behind the question. Answer the real question. Say, "My partner's in Podunk, but that will not affect my work here. I make a separation between work and personal life."

Be prepared for LDR-related questions during an interview. Your love life and family life are off-limits as considerations that determine whether or not you are hired, but interviewers may innocently venture into these areas. Have brief but honest answers ready that cut off the topic and allow you to move on. Remember, you are the subject of the interview, not your significant other. Your first objective is to get the offer. After you get it, you can judge whether to inquire about family-friendly policies.

Cracking the Whip on Yourself?

"My life consists of apartment, department, apartment, department," said a friend of mine who was in an LDR. She'd become terribly isolated, but had recognized it and forestalled a descent into despair by reaching out. In Chapter 13, I called this work-home routine tunnel vision, something that afflicts many LDR couples during their time apart. It can exacerbate workaholism in those who already have it and create it in people who do not naturally tend toward it.

It's Easy to Overwork

Have you ever noticed that work can expand to fill whatever time you have available for it? If there are five tasks and you have one day to do them, you'll do them in one day. But if you have those same five tasks and one week to do them, they somehow *require* the entire week. Since LDR partners often have nothing to go home to, they consider their evenings "available," and work can expand to fill the time. If this describes you, remind yourself of how many other things you could be doing each evening instead, that could enrich and fulfill you. Besides enriching your social life, arranging to go out with a colleague after work is a simple way to provide yourself with an incentive to finish your work and leave the office at a reasonable hour.

What about those who are efficient with time? Even with this trait, workaholism can be exacerbated. After all, work is likely the reason you're in your LDR in the first place, right? So spending extra hours at work is easy to justify. Kathy, for example, is a self-confessed workaholic. With a job in Sydney and a partner in Indiana, it was easy for the tendency to intensify. It ate up her life. "In the hotel industry," she said, "your desk is constantly filling up. I'd want to clear my desk before leaving for the day, but it was actually an impossible task. I'd end up working really late every day trying to do it." Kathy's work habits took their toll in the form of an uncontrollable twitch in her left eye. "I couldn't stop it, and kept worrying that people would think I was winking at them," she said.

 Survival Kit _____

Instead of allowing work time to become open-ended, try to keep regular work hours, even if they are *longer* work hours. This will keep your LDR travel- and work-rhythms sustainable.

She would take walks alone at night to let off steam. "I'd walk by the edge of the cliff [in Sydney], find a rock to sit on and just bawl," she said. "It helped me vent a little." In the end, she had to pull back for her own sanity. If you work many extra hours simply because there's no natural end to each day's work, set limits and pull back, as Kathy did.

Finally, work can be used to fill a personal void. There's nothing to go home to, and work provides easy meaning to life. Avoid the easy temptation to use work to fill a personal void, and direct energy to friendships and your social life, as described in Chapter 15. Apart from relationships, developing good "alone" skills, where you use solitude to recharge your batteries, can also offset overwork and workaholism.

Hit Your Stride

Sometimes it's nice to allow some aspects of life to just go the way they are going, without excessive attempts to manage everything. So, I will not blame LDR partners for overworking to fill the time available.

But here's a thought: In Chapters 10 and 15 I spoke of the benefits of keeping your LDR visits rhythmic and predictable. If you achieve such regularity with visits, then it's *possible* for your work life to become regular as well. Keeping regular work hours frees up time to develop other facets of your life. Keep that in mind. Even if you work late on weekdays to make up for LDR-related lost time, maybe those late hours can nevertheless be *regular* hours. Similarly, if you come in on weekends, maybe you can decide which weekend day it will be, and for how long. That way, you can use the remaining hours to build a life outside work even when you and your partner are apart.

The Least You Need to Know

- Establish your worth at work and develop a good relationship with your bosses and colleagues before you discuss your LDR with your boss.

- A family-friendly workplace can offer many options for someone in an LDR; when the time is right, explore these options with your supervisor.

- Be prepared for LDR questions during a job interview and answer them briefly but honestly.

- Avoid the tendency to overwork. Direct energy to your relationships and other facets of your life, so that you do not seek fulfillment solely through work.

Part

Taking Charge

Did you ever feel that your LDR just sort of swept you along? If you did, well, it's time to take charge. How can you tell if your LDR is working for you and your loved ones? We'll observe and feel out your LDR, with a little help from Aristotle. If you're ready for a change, and ready to end the distance, well, you have many decisions to make—but there's plenty of food for thought that you can feed on, and stories to help.

Chapter 18

Are You and Your Loved Ones Flourishing?

In This Chapter

◆ Assessing whether your LDR is working for you

◆ If you decide it's time to part

◆ Finding a way to flourish within the LDR

The *real* question is, are you happy? If the answer is yes, straight from the heart, without rationalizations and qualifications, then it hardly matters whether you're in an LDR or not, whether you live in Poughkeepsie and your partner lives in Timbuktu or not. If the answer is no, then perhaps it's time to figure out the reasons, and take charge of your LDR and life.

In this chapter, we'll take a step back and put the LDR in the context of a larger life so that you can assess it against the big picture. I'll first describe a framework for assessing how your LDR is working for you and your loved ones. Next, I'll examine options for taking charge if you decide that things are *not* working. The first involves ending the relationship, which LDR couples sometimes regretfully must do, just like any other couple. The second involves regaining your footing within your LDR to restore a state of flourishing. A third option for taking charge involves bridging the distance to live together. This option applies at any time you feel it's necessary, and I discuss this option in Chapter 19. If you're at a stage in your LDR where you want to evaluate it and come to some conclusions, this chapter will assist you.

A Framework for Flourishing

The question of how to live well within an LDR cannot be settled without some basic understanding of how to live well in general. Basic conditions for a good human life hold regardless of whether you are an LDR couple or a same-location couple. The advice in this book does not ignore these conditions, but rather is informed by them.

In a nutshell, it comes down to the much-mentioned concept of "balance." But what, we might wonder, does balance have to do with happiness and flourishing? Aristotle explained it first and explained it best, and the points that follow are based on his own.

Balance Inside and Out

Balance is not just about how you divide up your time. It's about your dispositions, and the actions that go with them. The reason that action in various spheres of human life—in ways that interest or challenge you and at a level sustainable over time—brings happiness is because the activity creates habits of thought and feeling that allow your personality to flower, and bring enjoyment.

> **Go the Distance**
>
> A summary of extremes that are self-destructive and balancing virtues that help us flourish can be found at www.molloy.edu/academic/philosophy/sophia/aristotle/ne2_notes.htm.

Living at extremes is sometimes enjoyable, but the problem is that extremes are unsustainable and harmful. Being consumed by one aspect of your life, profitable or fleetingly enjoyable though it may be at present, can drown out possibilities for fulfillment in other aspects of life and leave you feeling brittle, one-dimensional, and unhealthy.

It's because extremes are so harmful that excesses like gluttony and cruelty and deficiencies like stinginess and cowardice are called "vices." In the end, the goal of "balancing" brings us to some very old-fashioned results: it involves being good people, having virtuous dispositions, and living them out in our actions. (Incidentally, Aristotle considered, and I agree, that attending to your physical environment and your finances are elements of a balanced life just like the others.)

Typical Excesses in LDR Partners

We live in times when all kinds of extremes are quite common in society. And to compound the situation, the LDR lifestyle *lends* itself to certain extremes, magnifying the ones already present around us, and involving some that are common just in LDRs. If you've read the relevant chapters, you already know what they are. Workaholism is one extreme that is common in the LDR lifestyle. Unsociability or social isolation is another. Bad eating habits are a third. A substandard living environment is a fourth. There might be other extremes, of dispositions or behavior or both, in your own particular LDR, but if so you will have to identify them yourself!

The extremes that can manifest in LDRs come about for several reasons. First, they are easy to fall into because of the way time gets divided up in LDRs. Second, the very busy-ness that keeps us teetering on the brink of extremes prevents us from noticing them and checking ourselves. Third, we may not be in the habit of thinking of balance in terms of dispositions, moderation, virtues, and vice. Fourth, we may have forgotten that the whole point of our choices is for us and our loved ones to flourish, and because we've forgotten, we may continue with habits and decisions that have, over time, become harmful.

> **Travel Advisory**
>
> Some signs of workaholism are being constantly busy, feeling under pressure, finding it difficult to relax, being unwilling to take a vacation even though you need one, snatching meals while you work, and staying awake nights thinking about work or money. For suggestions on how to reduce workaholism, check out www.vernoncoleman.com/workaholic.htm.

If It's Time to (Regretfully) Part

If you examine your LDR and find that you and your loved ones aren't flourishing, you might decide it's because of the quality of your relationship. When LDR couples break up, the reasons that apply are likely the same as for other couples: lack of trust, lack of closeness, incompatibility, or breakdown in the face of the stress (which all couples, LDR or not, get tested by at some point, in some forms).

Here are some signs that may indicate that you're not flourishing within the relationship itself:

◆ The predominant feeling when you're with your partner is unhappiness, even though there may be nothing to point to, the sex may be fine, and both of you are trying.

◆ The predominant feeling in the relationship is indifference. You don't particularly look forward to seeing each other, talking, or communicating. The distance suits you quite well—the more distant, the better it suits. This indicates that the relationship, whatever it was before, may have become one of convenience.

◆ You don't really have a plan, or stated intentions, to be together. You *could* discuss it, but the opportunity doesn't propel either of you to do it. As a result, the relationship doesn't seem to have a future.

◆ You and your partner seem to be unequally committed. You do not feel cherished, but instead feel taken for granted or neglected, even after you've given avenues of long-distance communication plenty of chances to develop.

◆ You and your partner aren't able to develop trust with each other. You do not feel safe and nurtured within the relationship, and remain insecure even after giving the relationship lots of time to build trust.

If, for these or other reasons, you decide to end the relationship, keep in mind that breaking up is best done in person. It's the decent thing to do. It might be easier (for you) to do it over e-mail or the phone, but breaking up in person provides more closure for your partner. If you have to do it over the phone, wait until you can have a live conversation—don't leave a message on your partner's answering machine. Your partner may respond by proposing an immediate visit to discuss things. It would be considerate to allow your partner to have closure by agreeing to a meeting (assuming there's no threat, physical or otherwise, involved in that situation).

The aftermath of a breakup may be easier for LDR couples than same-location ones—one of those small mercies that may offer only miniscule comfort, but a mercy nonetheless. Both partners have a routine when apart from each other that remains unaffected by the breakup (barring the daily communication that may have been your habit, which you could miss acutely). So, though the end of the relationship may leave you hurting, you can find comfort in a daily routine that did not involve the other person's presence anyway. If you distract yourself with some activity when you would normally have had a phone call to look forward to, the pain of transition can be eased.

Regaining Your Footing

If you remain firmly committed, but find that you and your loved ones are *not* flourishing, it's time to regain your footing. Perhaps your LDR will continue a bit longer because you have a fixed time frame for it, and you've agreed to let it go on till then; or if you're in the middle of developing projects or accomplishing goals, and there's an anticipated or hoped-for win-win solution at the end of it. Whatever the reasons, if you are ready and willing to continue the LDR despite feeling a bit worn out, you're a trooper. Here (in addition to the advice in the rest of the book) are some ways to regain your footing and approach the remainder of your LDR time.

> **Go the Distance**
>
> Aristotle, in his *Nicomachean Ethics*, and C. S. Lewis, in his book *The Four Loves*, emphasize the importance of friendships in a person's life. (See Appendix A for details on both books.)

Stay Vigilant About Balance

Remain mindful of the fact that the LDR lifestyle makes it easy to drift into extremes and requires conscious correction from you when that happens. Stay alert to this possibility. It's important to check yourselves when you're becoming unbalanced and correct your course. If you do, you can flourish in your LDR, just like successful military and civilian LDR couples that stay strong, committed, and joyful through their long-distance years.

Practice, Habit, and the Aristotelian Way

As I've said, being well balanced is a matter of creating the right habits and dispositions in oneself. If you tend toward extremes, regaining your footing is a matter of slow and steady change. Keep these tips in mind to move away from extremes and restore balance:

- Identify areas where you live at extremes, and where you would like balance.

- Don't expect to manufacture the right feelings, virtues, and dispositions right off the bat. Instead, concentrate on what's within your power: your actions. If you want to achieve balance or virtue, say, in how you navigate through phone conflict, begin by *imitation*. How would a virtuous person behave during such phone fights? The first time you imitate the person's behavior, it will feel uncomfortable. However, as you repeat the good behavior every time you fight, it will become easier and eventually become habit. When behaving well in a fight comes to you naturally, that is when you know you have mastered that virtue.

- If you're cutting back on some extreme, give yourself a more attractive alternative. For example, if you recognize yourself as a workaholic who uses work to fill empty evenings, make cutting back on work attractive by arranging something you can look forward to in that extra time. Do you have an interest that you can give yourself permission to indulge, like music, reading, or playing a sport?

- Set realistic goals for cutting back on extremes and regaining balance. Radical changes are unlikely to last—you may succeed for a few days and then slip back worse than ever, and feel bad. Remember, you are creating *habits*, and these involve repeating the desirable behavior until those behaviors feel natural, good, and pleasurable.

Besides these general points, the specific advice in each chapter will aid with nuts and bolts of doing well in various areas of your LDR lifestyle. With practice, you can turn your long-distance lifestyle into a kinder, gentler thing, and yourself into a softer, less-driven person, and you can begin to flourish within the LDR lifestyle.

Surrendering Control (Over Some Things)

Well-adjusted military couples (we met some in Chapter 9) have a healthy attitude toward what they can control and what they cannot. Since they knowingly sign up for military life, they agree, *in advance*, to give up control of where they live, where they are sent for a mission, and for how long they are separated. Since they regard these things as given, beyond their control, they instead focus on what they *can* control. This becomes a habit, and if you ever meet a self-described "military brat," you'll likely observe the adaptable attitude ingrained during growing years.

In civilian LDRs, because partners often *find* themselves apart without knowing in advance that prior commitments and ties would lead to long distance, we keep feeling that we *ought* to be able to change things. We put a lot of pressure on ourselves, and accept pressure from friends and family, to *fix* what is perceived as needing fixing. As a result, we can become despondent when we encounter delays and obstacles.

 Survival Kit

If your LDR will continue for a few more years, decide that you will be adaptable, and surrender control of many things that you usually seek to control. Focus on your positive attitude, and adopt a proactive approach to deal with practical and pragmatic matters within your control.

If your LDR is going to continue for a bit, regard it the way healthy military couples do. It takes the pressure off. As Veronica, a military spouse of 13 years with two children, described her attitude: "We don't control things in life anyway. It's in our culture to have controlling personalities who feel they must control what happens to them. But not being able to control things is a given. The only thing you can control is your own attitude. My approach is to be open to what the universe has to offer, and make the best of the present circumstances." This spiritual attitude of surrender helps Veronica to trust that her life has direction through all the changes. Adopt Veronica's attitude: trust that you will take steps to be together at some point, but cannot do it right now.

Maintaining a Proactive Attitude Toward Other Things

Once you regard the LDR as a *given*, beyond your control at least for the moment, you can put your energy where it helps: your practical, day-to-day challenges and your attitude.

With practical, day-to-day tasks, be proactive. Break down overwhelming challenges into manageable chunks, so that you do not get consumed. If you have job searching, moving, projects, child rearing, or whatever, to do, prioritize. Ask, "What amount of this huge responsibility can I take a bite out of right now?" Then, when you've taken one bite, ask, "Okay, I sold the house/packed my stuff/organized my finances/whatever; what next?" This helps you establish control over the things that you *can* control on a practical and pragmatic level.

There are several ways to maintain a proactive attitude in your LDR. Staying positive is one part of it. As Veronica says: "It takes the same amount of energy to look at things positively as it takes to look at things negatively." I would even err on the side of saying that focusing on the positive requires less energy and yields greater rewards than focusing on the negative. (For instance, a negative attitude keeps you preoccupied with problems. Pulling out of that state helps you be more present in your immediate environment, and notice opportunities for any real solutions that present themselves.) It's just that negative things have a strange power to transfix us. If your LDR is going to continue, watch out for this tendency, and focus on what's working. Incidentally, by "stay positive," I don't mean adopt a fake chirpiness that will only wear you out and get on everyone else's nerves. I mean pull back your energies from wherever they are being squandered, reach within, and remind yourself of all that is good about the choices and actions within your LDR.

Deciding to be flexible is another aspect of maintaining a good attitude. As Veronica puts it, "The key is adaptability. When changes happen, you may be kicking and screaming, but it helps to decide at some point, 'Okay, I'm going to be a chameleon, I'm going to adapt, I'm going to find opportunities.'" The decision to be uncomfortable if necessary helps you tolerate discomfort with more grace.

Finally, remembering past challenges that you have overcome helps your present attitude, too, especially when you falter. Pam, in her younger years, earned her Master's degree over a decade while working full-time and raising children as a single mom (before she met and married John). She's the first in her family to have achieved this level of professional success. "I never get overwhelmed with what I am doing," she said, "because I think back to when I was working full-time, going to school and raising my children on my own, and know that that period was a much greater challenge than anything I'm now doing. Since I succeeded with *that* challenge, I can easily enjoy this one." Like Pam, keep your successes in mind, to give yourself a boost.

The Least You Need to Know

◆ Assess whether you and your loved ones are flourishing in different spheres of life as you maintain your LDR.

◆ If you're not flourishing within the relationship and decide to end it, keep in mind that an in-person breakup allows more closure.

◆ If you remain firmly committed but must continue for a while in the LDR, work to regain balance in the areas where you have tended toward extremes.

Chapter

Taking Charge of Your Life

In This Chapter

- ◆ Experiences that say you're ready for change
- ◆ Turning assumptions on their head
- ◆ Creating new possibilities to bridge the distance
- ◆ Building your courage with small steps

If you come to a crossroads, you will either take opportunities that require more long distance, or feel that it's time to live with your partner, and forego them. These are highly personal decisions. I know from my experience as an academic that there is often little wiggle room for couples. However, as we saw in Chapter 18, there are ways to seize the initiative to flourish within your LDR if it is going to continue for a while.

If you feel it's time to bridge the distance and live with your partner, what then? In this chapter, we'll discuss how to seize the initiative to make such a change successfully. Any idea how you will do it? Me neither. There is no one answer to fit everyone's situation.

However, starting now, I want you to believe in something: *the possibility of creating something new.* Certain answers come only when you're ready to ask new questions. When you put it out there that you're ready for change, well, you never know what might happen. My bet is that opportunities will appear from within and without, like invisible ink revealing its secrets. I'll ask some questions and tell some stories to show what I mean and get you thinking. You take it from there with your own questions, and your own story.

Why You Might Feel Ready for Change

Here's an analogy with milk, of all things. If you've ever boiled milk, you know that it can heat quietly on a back burner for a long time, so gently that you forget to watch it. But when it's hot enough, when you least expect it, it rapidly comes to a boil, foaming and demanding immediate attention. Your LDR can have a similar history. Slow changes can remain just below your conscious awareness for a long time, and then, at some unexpected moment, surge to the surface, demanding action. Let's examine some of the background "slow cooking" conditions that can set the stage for eventual action toward living together.

A Shift in Priorities

The realization that work has swallowed up the rest of life is not unique to LDR partners, but it can hit them more poignantly because LDR partners make greater sacrifices on the family front for work, literally through geographic separation.

For many LDR partners, what felt like an acceptable compromise at the beginning of the LDR can start to feel different after several years. The LDR often begins because there were certain opportunities—opportunities that imposed distance on partners—that had to be taken to fulfill prior educational, career, and financial commitments. But after several months or years in an LDR, those opportunities may have been taken, and the gains assessed. After some time, with the necessary experience of the LDR behind them, partners sometimes reassess their priorities, and find that their priorities tend toward family more than toward work.

Joan, in a 15-year military LDR, described this kind of changing priority toward family when she spoke of her active-duty husband, Mike: "He used to put work first, and everything else followed. But now I think family is becoming more important to him. I saw it most clearly during his last R&R break, when he wanted to spend a lot of time with the children and really cherished them. He has a choice, when his current agreement with the army is over, of whether to continue for a few more years or not. I think he may opt out."

> **Survival Kit** _____
>
> Changing priorities over time may motivate you to "do" the LDR differently (as described in Chapters 11 and 18), or seek new compromises to be together that may not have been available or realistic when the LDR first began.

The End of Wanderlust

Another possible change over time involves restlessness, or rather, the end of it. Moving around a lot can be habit forming. Many people, in the military and in academics, dislike relocation, but at the same time, come to expect it. So after a few years in one place, restlessness seizes them and they feel like starting fresh elsewhere. The thought of settling down in one place year after year after year can be a bit horrifying at a certain stage of life. However, this wanderlust can subside after several years in an LDR, and priorities can change toward partner, family, having babies, or enjoying children and grandchildren.

A Natural Movement Toward Resolution

Partners in dating LDRs can have a natural impulse to eventually bridge the distance. This impulse existed even in Jack, who loved the long-distance aspects of his relationships, and reveled in the opportunities for compartmentalization that they offered him. Even he says, "I would inevitably want the relationship to go to some kind of next level—want it to head somewhere. The compartmentalization of different aspects of my life was great for a long time [three to four years in each case], but at some level, I wanted to learn how to resolve differences and learn how to live together."

The "where is this relationship going?" question is typical even among same-location couples, and it naturally exists for LDR dating couples, too. Thus, couples in long-term dating LDRs often feel a natural progression in the relationship toward living together. If your dating LDR is like this, then you will find your priorities changing with time: changing, that is, toward making the necessary compromises to live together. At the very least, you might want to take the time to live together for a year or so before deciding whether or not your relationship is permanent, and whether or not it will involve a long-term LDR.

Loved Ones Flourishing, or Not?

Finally, there is the effect the LDR has over time on people you love, most notably your partner. Much depends on the expectations and personality of each partner and the nature of your LDR. Though LDR partners may gamely and uncomplainingly adjust to the situation, it may become wearing after many years, especially if your schedules do not permit regular and predictable visits and communication. If you see a sadness gathering around your partner, you may feel responsible for it and, out of love, want to come to a resolution. If that's the case—if it is sadness that gathers around one or both of you over time, rather than joy—you might start feeling that it is time for the LDR to end and for both of you to live together.

Factors That Precipitate Change

What I described earlier are some of the "slow-cooking" conditions that set the stage for bridging the distance. Now let's look at some "coming to a boil" experiences that tend to precede the actual decision to bridge the distance. Such experiences make you *notice* that you are quite ready for a big change, and take action. Let's look at the stories of some couples, to illustrate. See if you can relate to any of their experiences.

Job Without Fascination, Travel Without End

Dan found that his job as an engineer in an Illinois firm did not enthrall him. As a result, at some point it was easier to leave his life in Illinois and join Erica in Colorado. "The long-distance relationship didn't affect my job satisfaction," he said, "but the job dissatisfaction made it easier to decide to chuck it all and move."

The precipitating event, the one that preceded the actual move, happened one Christmas. Dan was at a Chicago airport to catch a flight to Colorado, where Erica awaited him. However, all flights were canceled. This was the third such snowy Christmas affecting Dan and Erica's Christmas reunion. The screens were blank because all of the airline's computers in Denver were down, so there was no information on the displays. "I looked outside at the snowplows, and inside at the blank displays, and thought, 'It's time to make a decision.'" Dan quit his job, sold his condo, and moved into Erica's trailer in Colorado—with no job lined up, but with a fiancée waiting for him. A new job followed soon enough.

> **Survival Kit** _____
>
> When it is time to seize the initiative and bridge the distance in your LDR, you will know it. Many milestones, experiences, and precipitating factors might be necessary before that moment arrives. Trust your instincts to signal when the time is ripe for change.

Job Not as Expected, Happiness Gut Check

My academic job made me reevaluate my career as well. I enjoyed teaching and interacting with students, but since I had 120 to 160 students a semester, I seemed to spend most of my time grading. I missed the camaraderie and socializing that had been plentiful in graduate school, but was lacking among professional academics in many (but not all) departments. Finally, the logical rigor required in my field seemed to bring out my combative tendencies and subdue my creative ones, which I did not like. The flourishing life I gravitated toward seemed hindered, rather than helped, by my experience of my work environment, and, after two years on the tenure track, I questioned whether I was doing what I loved. Like Dan, the LDR did not affect my job perceptions, but my job perceptions set the stage for changes to the LDR.

The precipitating moment for me came one day when I was on the phone with a college friend from India who was settled in the United States. "Oh Seetha!" she burst out, apropos of nothing, her voice positively thrumming with joy, "I'm so happy!" It struck me that I could not make such a ringing declaration about myself. I wondered why not, and the answer soon came: Over the years, Dave had become my most trusted friend. Seven years of an LDR, and the challenges Dave and I had faced together in it, had made me feel more emotionally close to him than ever. Besides, I'd always felt happiest and most buoyant when we were together. I hadn't felt ready, until now, to pay proper attention to these underlying facts. Now that I had achieved a milestone in my career, after years of training for it, I felt ready the minute I paused to take stock. So we made a plan to be together.

Change of Heart

Kathy's career in the hotel industry, which began when she was 24, was wonderful. "Working in the hospitality industry opened many doors and has great travel perks," she said. "I had no problem getting very involved in work." Kathy already knew she didn't want kids: "Motherhood didn't seem appealing after seeing the compromises my own mother made, and after seeing how other women my own age coped with motherhood." But over the years, and especially during her two years in Sydney, Kathy's feelings changed. She found that work had become too dominant. "I had too many late-night client dinners to count," she said, "often followed by early morning breakfasts or airport arrivals. My lack of leisure time combined with a stressed-out personality did not exactly help in the romance department!"

The precipitating factor came when she met her now husband, Tim, on a visit to the United States. "Having someone to share my life certainly was a good accelerator. To say that it was love at first sight would be too strong, yet I knew that Tim had the qualities I was looking for in 'the one'. Meeting him was a gentle reminder— no, actually, it was a lightning bolt— that one of my desires was to marry and have a family. At age 39, the time was *now*." So after a long-distance courtship, Kathy and Tim discussed how they would bridge the distance and live together.

> **Go the Distance**
>
> An inspiring book of stories about turning points in people's lives can be found in Po Bronson's book, *What Should I Do With My Life? The True Story of People Who Answered the Ultimate Question* (see Appendix A). Mr. Bronson also maintains a website based on his book at www.pobronson. com.

A Note on Gradual Change

Many couples have no precipitating factors. Sometimes, the original hope—that a combination of luck, diligence, and favorable circumstances will bring them together—works out, and they end up together. It can happen to academic couples, and it can happen to other couples. It happened, for example, for Josh and Marina, whose story I'll tell later in this chapter. If you are placing your hopes on such a resolution, rock on, but if the LDR is wearing you out, then consider putting a cap on how long you will wait for these wonderful but nebulous factors to come together for both of you.

Questioning Assumptions

Many professions depend on you being a rule-follower—that is, on following a well-defined and predictable course for advancement in that profession (if you do A, B, and C, then one day X, Y, and Z will follow). And, even if we don't think of ourselves as rule-followers, we accept many assumptions about the way things work, without question. Are there are assumptions involved in your lifestyle? Probably. Observe yourself and the people you interact with; you may be surprised. Once you articulate your assumptions, you will also be able to question many of them.

Consider Getting Off Track

Careers in education, the military, symphony orchestras, the government, corporations, and most other lines of work have their paths toward career advancement, a "track" if you will. In my profession, it is actually *called* a track: the "tenure-track." The progression is predictable: a Master's, a Ph.D., several one-year positions that send people hopping all over the country (trying madly to publish all the while), and then the holy grail of the tenure-track professor job for a

> **Travel Advisory**
>
> Beware of the belief that thinking outside the box and adapting to change applies only to the workplace. It serves business to encourage innovation and adaptability. The lessons are valuable, but remember, they also apply to your personal life, and can be used to create a solution to bridge distance between LDR couples.

fortunate minority every year. After all that work to get here, well, we'd better stay a while. If we stay diligent, we will advance. However, as one half of an LDR partner, you might have some incentives to look beyond the expected career track of your job. These things are not typically designed for the convenience of lovers who are separated by distance.

In business, we're regularly encouraged to think outside the box. I think that's great. Questioning how things are supposed to work helps innovation and adaptability. But remember to apply these creative attitudes from the work world to your personal life as well. Maybe you can create new solutions toward being together.

Turning the Tables on What's Negotiable

Being adaptable for the sake of your career is probably the very reason you're in an LDR. Right? At the end of Chapter 2, I laid out an assumption pointed out by some LDR researchers, and I'll review it again here. The assumption is that the demands of work are non-negotiable, and the requirements of family are flexible. That's why the LDR arises in the first place. You and your partner have decided to be adaptable to meet the requirements of one or both of your jobs.

I think adaptability is a great thing. It helps you survive and meet the challenges that come your way. However, this particular adaptability, which involves accepting the assumption that the demands of work are non-negotiable and the requirements of family life must bend in response, can contribute to increasing work-dominance in your life at greater and greater expense to family life.

Incidentally, this assumption is not peculiar to LDR couples. It's not as if same-location couples had it right all along, and can wag their fingers at you and say "I told you so," upon reading these paragraphs. Same-location couples accept the same assumption; it just manifests in long hours and stressful lifestyles of a different sort. The assumption is peculiar to modern life, exacerbated by businesses becoming more global and fast-paced, and professions becoming more specialized. If you're at a point where you've achieved enough in your profession to feel confident about it, and are sensing increasing work-dominance at too great a personal expense to you, this is the assumption to invert.

Once you're ready to invert the assumption, you might discover that the only reason work demands are non-negotiable is because you haven't negotiated them. You've accepted the conventional wisdom. What if you said to yourself, '*Here* are some personal boundaries, some requirements of mine for family life, which I will no longer negotiate. *These* are, for my purposes, inflexible.' It's a question of emphasis. As long as you emphasize the non-negotiable character of work, the degree of your adaptability for it can be endless, at greater and greater personal cost. But if your emphasis turns to your personal requirements for family life, and you start considering *them* non-negotiable, you may find that your professional life is more adaptable than you think. New, creative options can occur to you, and your career path can bend around your non-negotiable personal life. Question the assumption that has gone unexamined, and turn it on its head.

Creating Possibilities

I do not have an answer for your specific situation. However, this section can set you thinking about what's within your power, by showing you how others bridged the distance when they were ready.

Speaking Your Truths at Work

If you like what you are doing, you probably have nice bosses. When you are at a turning point, you might be ready to do what you've never done before: calmly speak to your nice bosses about your non-negotiable wants and desires, and state your desires for changes to your job. This can involve more risk than discussing the options for flexibility mentioned in Chapter 17. If you're at a point where you have certain non-negotiable requirements, you may have no idea whether your bosses will say, "Sorry, I cannot help you," or even, "Sorry, I have to let you go." So you have to be ready to walk away from your job if your requirements cannot be taken seriously. (This is where having one year's worth of money to live on stashed away, which I mentioned in Chapter 11, can come in handy.) Here are three stories about how things worked out.

"I Want to Live in the United States"

Here's what Kathy did: she walked into her bosses' office, and said, "When my Australian visa comes up for renewal, I would like to not renew. I want to live in the United States," Kathy had no idea how her bosses would react. Well, they thought that Kathy being in the United States and still working for them was a *great* idea. You see, Kathy was in charge of the North American clients of the Australian branch of an international hotel chain. When she traveled from Sydney to the United States, it was to see these clients. No one had proposed having the Sydney-employee-with-North American-clients live in North America rather than Sydney. The possibility only occurred to Kathy's bosses when Kathy declared her intentions.

> ### Go the Distance
>
> If you would like to explore what can be accomplished via telecommuting before you approach your boss and colleagues about it, check out www.langhoff.com/faqs.html.

"Well, okay, we will send you to Chicago," said her bosses. Chicago was the location of the hotel chain's branch office. Kathy discussed this proposal with Tim, and they considered it. It would mean a new LDR, but now in the same country. They did not want that. So Kathy went back to her bosses, and said that she wanted to live with Tim in Indiana. They tried to persuade her to go to Chicago. She finally said, "I'm not doing this for [hotel chain], you know. I'm doing this for my personal life. If it's not okay with you, that's fine, but I will still be going ahead with it." Well, Kathy's bosses worked with her. They agreed to allow her to work out of home in Indiana, operating a "satellite office." She has a weekly conference call with the Sydney office over the phone, and travels within the United States to meet the same clients as before. Home, however, is with Tim. It's worlds apart from their previous situation.

A Boss Who Takes Care of You

If you recall, Josh's job was in New York City, and Marina lived in Boston. Since Marina had relocated three times to be closer to Josh, she had made it clear that the next relocation, if it happened, would not be from her. Josh loved his job and he loved his boss. He'd made no secret of his LDR, and so his bosses and colleagues knew about Marina.

When Josh was snowbound in Boston, he often interacted with the office via e-mail, so his office already accommodated his LDR in many of the ways described in Chapter 11.

One day, Josh's boss approached him with an offer: He wanted to send Josh to Arizona to lead a project. However, he knew Marina was in Boston. He offered Josh a choice between either moving to Arizona, or moving to Boston to a branch office and *traveling* to Arizona every week. Josh's boss, whom Josh liked so much, was himself moving to the Boston branch office.

Well, you can imagine that Josh took the offer. "I was reaching a point in our relationship where, if something like this hadn't come along, I would have taken things into my own hands and made my wishes known to my bosses. But I have a good boss, the kind who considers his employees his greatest asset. He considers our happiness important." Josh trusted his boss, and his boss came through. Josh moved to Boston, and traveled to Arizona every week until the project was completed. The boss's investment in Josh's happiness also paid off for Josh's boss. When the latter moved to another Boston company, Josh followed. And when Josh's boss invited him to follow him to California, Josh and Marina both agreed. They were ready for some sun. Now, Josh and Marina are probably suntanned and smiling.

Wiggle Room in Academics

In my case, I made an appointment to see my associate dean, a lady I liked. When we met, we exchanged pleasantries, and then I said, "I need to either quit, or get a leave of absence." I had no idea if the latter was possible, but I wanted to let her know that I was thinking of leaving, and why. I told her my reasons: the commute, the desire to reclaim my enjoyment of writing, the desire to have *time* to write, and the desire to be with Dave. In my heart, I hoped I had options to buy time without burning bridges, but if not, I was psychologically prepared to leave.

She looked taken aback, but immediately said, "We can do a leave of absence!" Apparently, such possibilities were written down in official documents somewhere, and leave could be granted at the discretion of the administration without me even having to give exhaustive reasons. "What if I take a leave of absence, and don't want to come back?" I asked, knowing I'd already received good news and wondering if this question would prompt a reversal, but wanting to be up front. "Well," she said carefully, "We know that can sometimes happen. If we grant a leave of absence, we would *hope* that you plan to return. If you want to extend your leave to two years, which is usually no problem, or plan to not come back, you must give us plenty of notice."

It turned out that an unpaid leave of absence would not inconvenience the university, since a qualified teacher could easily be found to fill in for me. It would postpone my time to tenure if, and when, I returned, but that was fine with me. When I met with the Dean to make my request official, he greeted me jovially and said, "I'm in the happiness business. Didn't you know? It's no problem for you to take leave for a year or two, and figure out your plans. I did long distance with my wife too, for many years. I know how it is." He said other nice things, and I left relieved and impressed. Well, who would have thought!

Making a Plan

I hope these stories have inspired you and shown what can happen when *you* consider your relationship non-negotiable. Often your bosses and colleagues will be willing to accommodate your priorities, but you won't know unless you speak up. The events described in the stories are, incidentally, the *result* of plans, rather than a beginning of them. You and your partner, too, can make a plan before you begin to explore possibilities. Here are some elements to consider.

The Plan Must Work for Both of You

Being together should not involve the expectation that the woman in a relationship will drop everything and join her man, nor that she should be the one who makes all the compromises. You're both bright, and so require conditions that allow both of you to flourish. Your solution may require that *both* of you be willing to make professional, geographic, and personal changes. For example, Kathy's and Tim's plan involves give and take in two steps. The first step was for Kathy to move to Indiana to join Tim, which she has done. However, the quiet town where Tim lives doesn't suit Kathy after her fast-paced, vibrant life. So, the second step is for them to move to a bigger city after Tim's daughter (from a previous marriage) graduates high school in a few years. As you can see, this plan involves Kathy accommodating Tim, and he, in return, being willing to make changes to create a "win" situation for her.

Discover What You Really Want

The first step in planning for change is to discover what you want. You might want different things now than you did a few years ago. You might want to use the skills you have developed in your present career in a new one. You might want to take seriously a childhood dream about what you wanted to do when you grew up, that you never took seriously at the time. You might want children. You might want to live in a certain kind of town or city. Since this stage of planning involves just identifying wants, you do not have to impose constraints on yourself like "this one is *realistic*, that one's not." You'll eventually get practical, but not at this stage. So identify what you really want, free from constraints.

Now Attend to Nuts and Bolts

As far as nuts and bolts for your planning phase, consider the following steps:

1. Create a folder and give it a name (one long-distance couple in this book called theirs "Project Live Together").

2. Identify and communicate what each of you wants: the skills that you would like to use in your professional life; the steps you will need to take, if any, to develop new skills that you desire; how picky you are about where you live; what elements you would like in your work and personal environments; the cultural resources you would like to have available to you; the pace of life that you individually desire, and so on.

3. Think about where you're willing to compromise and accommodate each other, and where one person's priorities are too important to dilute. Continue this process of give and take until you have identified criterion for living together that are acceptable to both of you. Finally, if this applies, identify the geographic areas that meet both of your requirements. Identify cities, do your

research, list the places in order of priority, and, if the features of your environment are important to you, book tickets for visits to these places to see if you really want to live in any of them.

4. Set aside a time each week to have a meeting and review your progress toward living together. If your visits are regular, you can meet in person. If your visits are irregular, have a regular meeting over the phone when you cannot meet in person. Deciding on the day and time in advance will allow you to mentally prepare, and spare you the anguish of waiting until you're both in the right mood for these matters.

5. At the end of every meeting, say what each of you will be doing to advance your project: what you will research, the contacts you will develop, the phone calls you will make, the papers you will write, the things you will mail off, or whatever. At the beginning of the subsequent meeting, review your progress since last week.

6. Keep records of your meetings. At first you might feel silly: You're not *business* partners, you're *life* partners. Precisely: You're *life* partners. You're taking that notion seriously by planning how to live together.

Survival Kit _____

Allow at least a year, perhaps more, for your plans to materialize from their point of inception. In the meantime, while your LDR is still going on, remember to sock away money steadily so that you can buy yourselves time for your win-win solution, if necessary.

Keep the process relaxed and don't force things. You are talking about emotional matters and possibly scary changes. Courage takes time to build up, and there will be occasional emotional walls. So avoid high-pressure seriousness. Crack open a bottle of wine, let the conversations get off track occasionally, and enjoy the excitement of driving your own life.

Forging Ahead

Of course, having meetings is not enough. You will have to rouse yourself and take steps. Meetings are not the beginning and end of it. That would be a drag. It will not do for one partner to be gung ho and the other not. It's wise to avoid putting one of you in the position of insti-gator and cheerleader while the other sits back. If you are dragging your heels, honestly examine the fears that are holding you back or keeping you apathetic, and be straight with your partner.

Keeping Your Counsel

You and your partner are in charge of this plan. There's no obligation to share it. It might suffice to tell family and friends that you're work-ing toward being together, and have a plan, but you're keeping it under wraps. Now is not the stage for anyone to throw cold water on your hopes. You actually have a shot at being together, and you must believe it's possible and keep your spirits high. If you have doubts about whether your plan will sound good to someone else, just keep it to yourself. If you have a gut feeling that someone would make a good sounding board, by all means confide in that person. You're in charge.

Finding Your Courage

Finally, here's how to find your courage. You begin by *doing*. If you don't feel too brave, or if, in fact, you feel completely craven, do not allow yourself or your partner to become paralyzed. Encourage each other to take small steps, small forays into new territory, so that it starts feeling less scary and more familiar. Push up against your boundaries in small ways. As you make it past each last known boundary, your confi-dence will build. Soon you will hit your stride, and your plan to live and flourish together will be underway!

The Least You Need to Know

- ◆ Decide to be proactive and adaptable if your LDR will continue for a while longer.

- ◆ When you are ready to make a change you will know it, so trust your instincts.

- ◆ Question your assumptions about the non-negotiable character of work and the flexibility of family and personal life.

◆ Make a plan with your partner to forge a win-win situation that allows you to live and flourish together; evaluate your progress with regular meetings.

◆ Find your courage by taking small steps; as you meet with success, your confidence will build and you'll hit your stride in navigating new and exciting territory.

Appendix A

Further Reading

This is not a comprehensive list of all the LDR-relevant books available to you. It is a list of LDR-relevant books that I also found to be well written and easy to read.

Aristotle, translated by D. P. Chase. *Nicomachean Ethics*. Mineola, NY: Dover Publications, 1998.

Bronson, Po. *What Should I Do with My Life? The True Story of People Who Answered the Ultimate Question*. New York: Random House, 2003.

Gerstel, Naomi, and Harriet Gross. *Commuter Marriage: A Study of Work and Family*. New York: Guilford Publications Inc., 1984.

Glass, Shirley, and Jean Coppock Staeheli. *Not "Just Friends": Rebuilding Trust and Recovering Your Sanity After Infidelity*. New York: Free Press, 2004.

Guldner, Greg. *Long-Distance Relationships: The Complete Guide*. Corona, CA: JF Milne Publications, 2004.

Lewis, C. S. *The Four Loves*. San Diego, CA: Harcourt, 1971.

Moore-Ede, Martin, Suzanne LeVert, and Scott Campbell. *The Complete Idiot's Guide to Getting a Good Night's Sleep.* Indianapolis: Alpha Books, 1998.

Sivananda Yoya Vedanta Center. *Yoga Mind & Body.* New York: DK Publishing, 1998.

Warner, Judith. *Perfect Madness: Motherhood in the Age of Anxiety.* New York: Riverhead Hardcovers, 2005.

Weschler, Toni. *Taking Charge of Your Fertility: The Definitive Guide to Natural Birth Control, Pregnancy Achievement, and Reproductive Health.* New York: Perennial, 2001.

Appendix B

Online Resources

This is not a comprehensive list of all the LDR-relevant websites available to you. It is a list of LDR-relevant websites that I also found to be helpful and user-friendly.

Communication

Calling plans:
www.calling-plans.com

Webcam options:
www.apple.com/ichat
http://home.core.com/web/technicalsupport/newuser/
communicate.html

Letter-writing:
www.wendy.com/letterwriting

Money

Money management:
www.personalmoneymgmt.com
www.microsoft.com/money/default.mspx
http://quicken.intuit.com/?src=www.quicken.com

Travel

Bus lines:
www.peterpanbus.com
www.greyhound.com

Noise cancellation headsets:
www.bose.com
www.amazon.com (electronics department)

Ergonomic driving:
www.drivingergonomics.com
www.worksafesask.ca/files/ont_ohcow/driving.pdf

Well-Being

Furniture rental:
www.rentfurniture.com
www.cort1.com

Sleep tape:
www.whitenoise.com

Caffeine addicts:
http://home.howstuffworks.com/caffeine4.htm

Yoga:
www.everythingyoga.com/studios.asp
www.yogajournal.com/newtoyoga/864_1.cfm#1

2005 food guide:
www.mypyramid.gov
www.mypyramid.org (a critical website)

Work

Balancing work and family:
www.labour.gov.sk.ca/family/INDEX.HTM

Telecommuting:
www.langhoff.com/faqs.html

Workaholism:
www.vernoncoleman.com/workaholic.htm

Friendship and Family

LDR discussion groups:
www.geocities.com/lysh19
http://groups.yahoo.com/group/WishYouWereHere

Trucker LDRs:
http://lists.topica.com/lists/TTCwomen

Family:
http://psychcentral.com/library/parents_kidsrel.htm

Finding Balance

Balance and extremes:
www.molloy.edu/academic/philosophy/sophia/aristotle/ne2_notes.htm

Military Couples

Deployment preparation:
www.afcrossroads.com/famseparation/predeployment_menu.cfm

Law that protects your job:
www.military.com/Resources/ResourcesContent/
0,13964,31004--0,00.html

Family Readiness Group info:
www.silentwarriors.net/frg4.html
www.vtguard.com/FamilyReadiness/How%20to%20start.htm

Domestic violence military assistance:
www.armycommunityservice.org/vacs_advocacy/data/modules/pbm/
rendered/spouse_abuse_1.asp

Comprehensive resources:
http://militaryspousemagazine.com
www.armyonesource.com
www.armycommunityservice.org/home.asp
www.silentwarriors.net/index.html

Appendix C

Real Advice from Real Couples

Several people shared their long-distance stories for this book. At some point, I asked each person with whom I spoke: "If you had to give one piece of advice to couples in long-distance situations similar to yours, what would it be?" Almost everyone had a response, and what follows are their own words. My own and Dave's words are included as well.

Dan (of Dan and Erica), LDR through dating and engagement, now married and living together for over a decade You must learn to trust one another and believe the two of you together can make it work. There is no room for possessiveness or jealousy. Most likely, many of your friends and relatives (perhaps insecure in their own relationships) will tell you it can't last. But it has worked for many others and it will for you, if you care enough for one another to make it so.

Joe (of Joe and Liz), Navy LDR of several years, married with young children You don't have to do it alone. There are many resources available out there for people who care enough about their relationship to keep it strong. Many people often feel alone and isolated. They also take a lot of abuse from family members who are quick to criticize and judge. This also adds to the confusion and depression that most people can feel when separated from their partner. "I told you this would happen!" is a common phrase from family members and, believe me, that only makes things worse. GET HELP! There are support groups out there with people in the same situation, and I don't believe they are too hard to find.

Josh and Marina, dating LDR for more than five years, living together as of 2004   There is no exact formula for making a long-distance relationship work. For us, frequent phone calls, e-mails, and letters seemed to be the best way to stay involved in the other person's daily life. We embraced each other's independence as a good thing, yet worked toward eventually being together. This made the distance stage in our relationship worthwhile and healthy as far as our individual development goes. Recognizing that it's not easy to be apart, if you care enough about the person, the relationship will work out.

Pam (of Pam and John), married LDR of more than five years, with adult children   The most important thing is communication. Communicate frequently so that you know what's going on in each other's lives. I don't mean just calling, I mean sharing what the day has been like. When you're at home, show interest in what your partner's been doing, and the same goes for your partner. The frequent communication when you're apart helps because you can show interest in what's been going on when you're together.

It's also important to do things together when you're at home. The time may be a squeeze, because visits are also the time for hair appointments, dentist appointments, etc., but make it a point to get out together, for instance for dinner, the theater, or time with friends.

Christine (of Christine and Ron), LDR through dating and engagement, now living together and married with children
Write lots of letters, the old-fashioned way. Staying in touch with not only each other but with your feelings on a day-to-day basis will strengthen your relationship. Saving the letters from your honey will give you something to look back at and ponder when you aren't together. Then, when you finally are living in the same space, you will have a tangible history of your relationship that will be priceless!

Ron (of Christine and Ron)   Being separated, it is hard to feel connected to the other person. You are missing the day-to-day things. It takes some effort to keep in touch so that each person still feels like they are a part of the other's life. Take advantage of the ways we have today to keep in touch: mail, e-mail, instant message, cell phone, text messages, whatever works for you. Once in a while, show up unexpectedly. One of my favorite memories was when Christine drove nine hours to surprise me for Valentine's Day.

Joan (of Joan and Mike), married dual-career army LDR for more than 15 years with young children   What helped me most were my friendships. I'd advise you to get out in the community, make friends, get involved and get your children involved in activities. Not being involved makes the time goes by slower. Being involved helps you keep your interests, and allows the time go by with a sense of normality. Keep up with the activities you had prior to separation as far as possible, and remember that your partner will be back with you one day.

Dave (of Dave and Seetha), LDR for seven years through engagement and marriage, living together as of 2004   At some point the distance will wear on you and you will wonder why you were so stupid as to choose this path. When that happens, remember that everyone makes choices and sacrifices. Couples living together make them too, even if they don't realize they are making them. You went into this knowing that there would be benefits and sacrifices: remind yourself about the benefits that you and your partner are enjoying in exchange for the sacrifices, and pat yourselves on the back for being fully aware that you were making an incredibly important decision about your lives.

Seetha (of Dave and Seetha)   I sometimes think that LDR partners take each other less for granted, and more fully appreciate the beauty of the other. There is a lot of love and kindness in the relationship, which you will keep even when the long distance ends and you live together. Cherish these rewards of your LDR. When you have distance between you, the quality, rather than quantity, of your relationship helps it endure. When you eventually live together you will have both, instead of swapping one for the other. Were it not for the experience of the LDR, this daily appreciation of the other might not have existed. Remember this, and you can find in the LDR a reason for gratitude, that such an opportunity has come into both your lives to develop a loving relationship.

Jack (of Jack and Lisa), four serious dating LDRs, married in 2005 and living with wife, Lisa   Weekend conflict in an LDR is a chance to identify and learn to work with differences. The important moments in the LDR are when differences show up. Honor the difference: Speak your whole truth, and listen completely to what the other has to say. It's your chance to ask, "Is this a difference I want to live with?"

Use the time in between to reflect on what is showing up about yourself in the relationship. Regard the respite as a time to do the sort of inner work you cannot do if you lived in the same place. If you live in the same city, you can get swept up by someone you're dating and lose your self. The rhythm of the LDR slows things down to a reasonable pace. Find out how to be yourself and heal yourself in the time that you're apart, and keep bringing a better version of yourself to the relationship during the times you're together.

Makoto and Chie, LDR through dating, engagement, and periods of marriage, living together as of 2004 with their infant son   We have not been in our relationship for too long, but we have one rule of thumb that we try to keep in mind, which works, we think, for any relationship, but especially long-distance ones. It is: "believe what you felt when you first met." We have experienced many irritations with each other and there will be more situations causing irritations. We believe, however, that we can get over them as long as we can remember the instinctive feeling we had when we met each other for the first time. That instinct brought us together, and we will stick with it.

Ariana (of Ariana and Claudio), two-year LDR through dating and marriage, living together as of March 2005   Be very clear about what you need and want from a relationship. I wanted distance because spending time alone is important to me. It is part of my nature. I fell in love with my husband, and we lived, at the beginning, on different sides of the ocean. It was romantic to be filled with such longing for closeness and to be unable to be together. If we engage in a long-distance relationship as a response to an inner need to maintain distance, I think that acknowledging that fact will help to manage so many details.

On a practical level, I would tell you to duplicate your personal environment in both places to avoid the frustration of not having the stuff necessary to be comfortable. Some things should not require thought. Don't add to the stress of transitions by neglecting important items necessary for taking care of yourself physically.

A long-distance relationship has prevented me from being able to fully live in each moment. It has been an avoidance strategy in many ways. When I am with my husband and things get tough, I can always go "home." And when I am feeling very lonely in my preferred state of aloneness, I can always go home to him. The question I would pose to you is: Is there enough of you to live two lives? In the end, I decided that I could not divide myself anymore. So I have quit my job, moved out of my apartment and returned to Lucca to live with Claudio. If I decide this is not what I want, then I will go live somewhere else—but completely somewhere else. No more divisions.

Veronica (of Veronica and Ed), married army LDR of 13 years, with young children   I encourage you to seek balance in your life, between the intellectual, the physical, and the spiritual. Nurture all three. Your life can go off-kilter if one of them is off. For instance, if you focus on career too much, or are emotionally extreme, the rest can suffer. When you forget your spiritual side, that's when things come tumbling down. Be mindful of each area and give attention to each one. A few minutes of prayer, meditation, or even hugging a tree—whatever expression you have for your spirituality—can work wonders. It's a small effort that has a phenomenal effect. You'll never have balance in a perfectionist sense, but you can have a moving fulcrum towards it—like a glass of wine that you keep moving in small circles to get the contents spinning, but not jerking or splashing wildly.

Kathy (of Kathy of Tim), LDR through dating, married and living together as of 2004   Hang in there if you feel the other person is "the one" for you; otherwise, don't waste your time!!! The stress of an LDR can be so great that you will feel like giving up at times, but follow your heart. If it is time to give up, or time for one of you to move to the other person's city, you will know. I would also advise against marrying the person too quickly after moving to the same city. Being in an LDR is a bit like being on vacation—only seeing someone on weekends and vacations is not "real life" and real life needs to happen before making a lifelong commitment.

Index

About the Author

Seetha Narayan has had seven years' experience in a long-distance relationship, and is intimately familiar with the insides of airports, highways stretching before her, lengthy telephone calls, and joyful reunions.

She has lived in many places. She grew up in India, in teeming, intense Bombay. Since moving to the United States, she has lived in the vast Midwest, the Rockies, the West Coast, and the vibrant East, often shuttling between two places to be with her fiancé and now husband, who similarly shuttled to be with her.

Since 2002, Seetha has been a professor of philosophy at a liberal arts college in Pennsylvania, teaching logic and ethics. She has a B.A. in sociology and a Ph.D. in philosophy. She was the grand-prize winner of the 2004 Memoirs Ink writing contest, has written for the journal *Social Philosophy Today*, and has presented her scholarship at conferences around the world.

At present, Seetha is taking a break from her job to be with her husband in Colorado, where she resides. When not teaching or commuting, she enjoys writing, hiking, playing board games, and spoiling her near and dear.